Exam Prep

encumber
subrogation
Rescrission
Novation
Hypothecation

duress

ANTHONY SCHOOLS®

A **Kaplan Professional** Company

ANTHONY SCHOOLS

A **Kaplan Professional** Company

5939 Balboa Avenue
San Diego, CA 92111

Exam Prep

Published by **ANTHONY SCHOOLS**, A **Kaplan Professional** Company
© 2003 Dearborn Financial Publishing, Inc.

ISBN 0793186900
PPN 64012901

DISCLAIMER
This material is for educational purposes only. In no way should any statements or summaries be used as a substitute for legal or tax advice.

10 9 8 7 6 5 4 3
Printed in the United States

Table of Contents

Personal Evaluation and Study Guide Worksheet

Examination: California Real Estate Salesperson

Prelim Score _____ Passing Requirement 53/75 Pass/Fail B 57/57

Screening Score _____ Passing Requirement 53/75 Pass/Fail B 57/57

Exam Section	Preliminary Exam					Screening Exam					Reference Pages		
	Very Weak	Weak	Average	Strong	Very Strong	Very Weak	Weak	Average	Strong	Very Strong	Principles Textbook	Principles Notebook	Power Test
Property Ownership, etc...	0-6	7-8	9-10	11-12	13	0-6	7-8	9-10	11-12	13	35-75 100-123 413-435	27-88 171-200	1-41 123-168
Laws of Agency	0-4	5	6-7	8	9	0-4	5	6-7	8	9	124-164	243-274	1-30 123-168
Valuation and Appraisal	0-4	5	6-7	8	9	0-4	5	6-7	8	9	357-386	201-242	1-30 69-83 123-168
Financing	0-5	6	7-8	9	10	0-5	6	7-8	9	10	209-269	291-356	1-30 53-68 123-168
Transfer of Property	0-3	4	5	6	7	0-3	4	5	6	7	76-99 270-322	127-170 357-390	1-30, 42-52 97-104 123-168
Practice of Real Estate	0-9	10-11	12-14	15-16	17-18	0-9	10-11	12-14	15-16	17-18	1-34 165-208 387-412	1-26 89-126 391-414	1-30, 84-96 105-122 123-168
Contracts	0-4	5	6-7	8	9	0-4	5	6-7	8	9	165-208 323-356	89-126 275-288	1-30 123-168

Content Specifications—California Real Estate Exam

- Property Ownership and Land Use Controls and Regulations
  (18% of Salesperson Exam, 15% of Broker Exam).
  - Classes of property
  - Property characteristics
  - Encumbrances
  - Types of ownership
  - Descriptions of property
  - Government rights in land
  - Public controls
  - Environmental hazards and regulations
  - Private controls
  - Water rights
  - Special categories of land
- Laws of Agency
  (12% of Salesperson Exam, 12% of Broker Exam)
  - Law, definition and nature of agency relationships, types of agencies, and agents
  - Creation of agency and agency agreements
  - Responsibilities of agent to seller/buyer as principal
  - Disclosure of agency
  - Disclosure of acting as principal or other interest
  - Termination of agency
  - Commission and fees
- Valuation and Market Analysis
  (12% of Salesperson Exam, 11% of Broker Exam)
  - Value
  - Methods of estimating value
- Financing
  (13% of Salesperson Exam, 13% of Broker Exam)
  - General concepts
  - Types of loans
  - Sources of financing
  - How to deal with lenders
  - Government programs
  - Mortgages/deeds of trust/notes
  - Financing/credit laws
  - Loan brokerage
- Transfer of Property
  (9% of Salesperson Exam, 10% of Broker Exam)
  - Title Insurance
  - Deeds
  - Escrow
  - Reports
  - Tax aspects
  - Special processes

- Practice of Real Estate and Mandated Disclosures
  (24% of Salesperson Exam, 27% of Broker Exam)
  - Trust account management
  - Fair housing laws
  - Truth in advertising
  - Record keeping requirements
  - Agent supervision
  - Permitted activities of unlicensed sales assistants
  - DRE jurisdiction and disciplinary actions
  - Licensing, continuing education requirements and procedures
  - California Real Estate Recovery Fund
  - General ethics
  - Technology
  - Property management/landlord-tenant rights
  - Commercial/industrial/income properties
  - Specialty areas
  - Transfer disclosure statement
  - Natural hazard disclosure statements
  - Material facts affecting property value
  - Need for inspection and obtaining/verifying information
- Contracts
  (12% of Salesperson Exam, 12% of Broker Exam)
  - General
  - Listing agreements
  - Buyer broker agreements
  - Offers/purchase contracts
  - Counteroffers/multiple counteroffers
  - Leases
  - Agreements
  - Promissory notes/securities

PROPERTY OWNERSHIP AND LAND USE CONTROLS AND REGULATIONS
(Salesperson 18%/27 questions; Broker 15%/30 questions)

PART I: Property Ownership

I. **CLASSES OF PROPERTY/REAL ESTATE AND PERSONAL PROPERTY**

    A. **Real Estate**

    Real estate includes land plus improvements plus appurtenances, which include rights, privileges and fixtures

        1. Land

            a. Surface rights

            b. Air rights

            c. Sub surface rights, including mineral, oil, and gas rights

        2. Improvements

            a. Items affixed to the land with the intent of being permanent

            b. Examples include a house, garage, fence, landscaping, etc.

        3. Appurtenances including rights, privileges and fixtures

            a. Fixtures are items that once were personal property but have been so affixed to real estate that they have become real property

                i. The legal tests of a fixture, in reverse order of importance, are: Method of Attachment, Adaptation, Relationship of the parties; Intent, Agreement

                ii. Emblements (crops) and trade fixtures are exceptions to the law of fixtures and are <u>personal property</u>

                    • Emblements are annually cultivated crops that belong to the party who rightfully planted the seed

                    • Trade fixtures are tenant-installed additions to a property for use in a trade or business

B. **Personal Property/Chattel**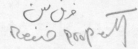

1. Everything that is not real estate; <u>movable</u> items

2. Personal property is transferred by a bill of sale (real property is transferred by deed)

C. **Personal Property Can Become Real Property and Vice Versa**

1. Personal property becomes real property by attachment

- <u>Accession</u> is the addition to real estate by attachment or accretion

2. Real property becomes personal property by severance

II. **PROPERTY CHARACTERISTICS**

A. **Physical Characteristics of Land**

1. Immobile – the geographic location of a piece of land is fixed

2. Indestructible – the long-term nature of improvements plus permanence of land tends to create stability in land development

3. Unique or nonhomogeneous – all parcels differ geographically and each parcel has its own location

B. **Economic Characteristics of Land**

1. Scarcity – although there is a substantial amount of unused land, supply in a given location or of a specific quality can be limited

2. Improvements – placement of an improvement on a parcel of land affects value and use of neighboring parcels of land

3. Permanence of investment – improvements represent a large fixed investment; land is not a liquid asset

4. Area preference, or situs – this refers to people's choices and desires for a given area

III. LEGAL DESCRIPTION

A. Methods of Legal Description

1. Metes and bounds - linear measurements, directions and degrees

    a. Begin and end at the Point of Beginning

    b. A monument is a visible marker, a natural or artificial object, used to establish the lines of a legal description

2. Rectangular survey/government survey – applies to over 30 states, especially in western U.S.

    a. Based on pairs of principal meridians and baselines governing the surveys in particular areas

        i. Principal meridians run North-South

        ii. Baselines run East-West

        iii. There are 3 Principal Meridians in CA

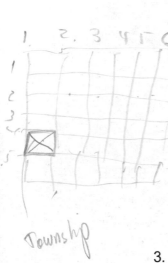

    b. The government survey method further breaks down areas into Townships; a Township is 6 miles x 6 miles (6 miles square; 36 sq. miles)

    c. Range - vertical rows of townships (north-south)

    d. Tier - horizontal rows of townships (east-west)

    e. A township contains 36 sections

    f. Section – 640 acres – 1 mile x 1 mile (1 mile square; 1 sq. mile)

    g. Acre - 43,560 square feet

3. Recorded map (lot, block, subdivision) - urban/residential

4. Informal reference - Street addresses are informal references that are not legal descriptions

Value of N½ of N¼ of Sec 6
80 ← 160 ← 640

43,560 —
Feet in Acres

Sample Question:

> Which of the following is the largest parcel of land?
> **a.** 5,280' x 10,560'
> **b.** 1/10 of a township
> **c.** 40 acres
> **d.** Two sections

B.   Survey

1.   Lender may require

2.   May reveal encroachments or zoning violation

IV.   TYPES OF OWNERSHIP – ESTATES AND ENCUMBRANCES

Both a tenant renting an apartment building and an owner of a house or condominium have estates in real property.

A.   Freehold Estates

1.   Fee simple absolute lasts forever and features the maximum control of use

     a.   Fully transferable and inheritable

     b.   Highest form of ownership in real estate

2.   Fee simple defeasible or determinable fee lasts "so long as" <u>condition</u> is met

     a.   Fully transferable and inheritable as long as condition is met

     b.   Violation of the condition can result in loss of title

3.   Life estate lasts for duration of a person's lifetime

     a.   Can be based on the life of the life tenant or on another person's life ("pur autre vie")

     b.   Life tenant has ownership and use; also has certain obligations

     c.   Reversionary estate – Grantor retains future interest at end of life estate

    d.   Remainder estate – If grantor transfers future interest

    e.   On death of life tenant, estate returns to fee simple

    f.   Lease by life tenant to another terminates upon death of measuring life

    g.   A life estate is not an "estate of inheritance" – a life tenant who is the measuring life cannot will the estate

B.   Less-than-Freehold (Leasehold) Estates

    1.   Estate/tenancy for years – Predetermined termination date; definite period; no notice required

    2.   Periodic estate/tenancy – Continues from period to period, such as month-to-month, until proper notice given. Renews under same conditions and terms upon payment of rent.

    3.   Estate/tenancy at will – Continues at owner's consent. CA has notice requirements

    4.   Estate/tenancy at sufferance – When a "holdover tenant" stays beyond termination without consent. If landlord accepts payments, becomes a periodic tenancy.

    5.   Lessee has a <u>chattel real</u>, a personal property interest in real property.

    6.   Lessee has a leasehold estate; Lessor holds leased fee estate and has a reversionary interest.

A Burden

C.   Encumbrances / Imperfections

A non-possessory interest in the lands of another. May create a cloud on title that may impair or lessen owner's rights.

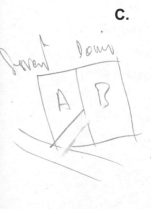

    1.   Easement – Non-possessory right to use the lands of another for a specific purpose

Run w/ the land

        a.   Appurtenant easement has a dominant tenement and a servient tenement

        b.   Easement in gross has no dominant tenement, only servient; e.g. utility easement

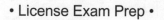

  c. Terminated by merger, release or abandonment

2. Deed restrictions/restrictive covenants/subdivision deed restrictions / condominium by-laws or CCRs (covenants, conditions, and restrictions)

Promise

  a. Privately created limitations on land use that protects property values and the interests of property owners

  b. Owners may be subject to <u>injunction</u> for violating covenants (Result of violating covenant is <u>not as harsh</u> as violating a condition)

3. Lien – claim that attaches to and is binding on property to secure debt repayment

  a. Property tax/special assessments – specific lien. Takes priority over all other liens, even those previously recorded

  b. Mechanic's – specific lien

    i. Priority dates to when work began or materials were delivered

    ii. Requires verification and recording for validity

  c. Mortgage or trust deed – specific lien

  d. Condominium/townhouse association – specific lien

  e. Judgment – general lien

  f. Attachment – a lien created against property before issuance of a judgment

(get a Survey)

4. <u>Encroachment - unauthorized use of another person's land</u>

  a. Survey points out

  b. Standard title insurance won't protect (requires <u>visual inspection</u>); <u>ALTA</u> insurance may cover

5. License – revocable permission to use the land of another without creating an estate in land

6.   Lis Pendens – A recorded document that gives constructive notice of a pending lawsuit

V.   TYPES OF OWNERSHIP

The manner of holding title has significant legal and tax consequences. An attorney specializing in such matters should be consulted. Licensees should NEVER advise on how to take title.

A.   Sole Ownership/Estate in Severalty

1.   When property is owned solely and separately by one person or one entity it is called <u>an estate in severalty</u>

2.   A corporation can hold title in severalty

B.   Concurrent Ownership

more than one person at the same time

1.   Tenants in Common - own undivided fractional shares with no right of survivorship. Each co-owner has <u>equal right of possession</u>

a.   Interests pass to <u>heirs</u> or <u>devisees</u> upon death

b.   Ownership shares do not have to be equal

c.   Co-owner can sell, lease, encumber, give away, or will share

2.   Joint tenants – co-ownership with the right of survivorship

a.   Upon death of co-owner, interest of deceased is dissolved and goes to <u>co-owner(s)</u> without delay of probate

b.   Four unities are required: Time, Title, Interest, and Possession (TTIP)

c.   Co-owner can sell, lease, encumber, give away share, but CANNOT will it

i.   If co-owner sells share, unities of time and title are disturbed; new co-owner holds title as tenant in common with other co-owner(s)

ii.   If co-owner encumbers share and defaults, foreclosure action will also disrupt unities; creditor will take title as tenant in common with other co-owners

        iii.   If co-owner encumbers share and dies prior to foreclosure action, creditor has no claim, since deceased's interest in land has dissolved

    d.   Can be terminated and property divided by partition suit

3.   Community property *married couples*

    a.   Husband and wife are equal partners in the community property – that property acquired during the marriage

    b.   Community property is an actual way of holding title; a deed stating that grantees take title "as husband and wife" will presume community property

    c.   Property acquired before marriage and property acquired after marriage by gift, inheritance, personal injury lawsuit, or if there is a written agreement, is separate property

    d.   Income from separate property remains separate property unless the finances are commingled

    e.   Recent law change allows for community property with right of survivorship

4.   In trust – ownership in a fiduciary capacity for another

5.   In Partnership

    a.   Pooling of resources to form an entity for the purpose of making and operating an investment – a syndication

    b.   A general partnership is an association in which all partners participate in the operation of the business and may be held personally liable for business losses and obligations.

    c.   A limited partnership or limited liability partnership (LLP) includes general partners (who run the business) as well as limited partners (sometimes called silent partners) who may be held liable for losses only to the extent of their investment.

    d.   May require securities license and be governed federally by SEC and locally under state Blue Sky Laws

VI. SPECIAL CATEGORIES OF LAND

A. Condominium

Air & Common Areas / Parcel

1. Real estate, portions of which are designated for separate ownership (units) and the remainder of which, <u>including the physical structure</u>, is designated for common ownership and use (common elements)

2. Fee simple interest in unit plus undivided interest in common elements as tenants in common transferred by deed

3. Each unit and its common element % is taxed, homesteaded, insured, and transferred as a separate parcel

4. Conversion is the process of changing from rental apartments to condominium ownership

B. Stock Cooperative

1. Ownership by a corporation, which in turn leases space to shareholders

2. Buyer receives corporate by-laws, shares of stock, and proprietary lease

3. Since there is no ownership of the unit, the buyer does not receive a deed

4. Owner pays assessments/association fees

180 | 90
Final Report

C. Community Apartment Project

1. Owner has an undivided interest in the entire property and a right to occupy a certain unit

2. Operation, maintenance, and control are usually exercised by a governing board elected by the owners

180 dys before sale the Tenant to move.
90 dys aftr the Fin Rpt c/ Tenant to buy.

Trustor / Trustee

D. **Time-shares**

    1.   A common interest ownership form where multiple owners have interest in a property

    2.   Each purchaser receives the right to use the facilities for a certain period of time each year

E. **Planned Unit Development (P.U.D.)**

    1.   Consists of separately owned parcels of land together with membership in an association which owns common areas. E.g., a gated community

    2.   Differs from a condominium in that the property owners actually own the land beneath their house, rather than the air space of the condo unit

<u>Note:</u> **Present tenants of a proposed condominium, community apartment project, or stock cooperative must be given notice of a right to purchase their units for 90 days after the issuance of the Public Report.**

PART II: Land Use Controls and Regulations

I. **GOVERNMENT'S RIGHTS IN LAND**

    A. **Collect property taxes and special assessments**

        1.   "Ad valorem" - "According to value"

        2.   May seize and sell by enforcing property tax lien

        3.   <u>Special assessments</u> are taxes levied against specific properties that benefit from a public improvement

    B. **Eminent domain**

        1.   Right to "take" private land for public use

        2.   <u>Condemnation</u> is the process *[handwritten: compensation]*

        3.   Fair compensation including property value plus damages

        4.   Inverse condemnation – an owner-initiated court action seeking the government to pay fair compensation when the owner's property has been substantially interfered with

    C. **Police power**

        1.   Enact and enforce laws governing land use to promote and support the public health, safety, morals and general welfare

        2.   Examples include zoning, building codes, subdivision regulations, safety codes, etc.

        3.   While zoning, etc. may affect property value, generally not considered a "taking" and requires no compensation

D.   **Escheat**

1.   Government's reversionary right

No Heirs

2.   Abandoned property or property of intestate owners with no heirs may revert to the government

II.   **ZONING**

A.   **Municipalities Structure Ordinances - Not State or Federal Government**

B.   **Typical Zoning and Land Use Classifications**

1.   Residential, Commercial, Industrial/Manufacturing, Agricultural, Mixed

- Codes based on these classifications: e.g. R3 is multi-family residential

2.   Buffer zone is an area of land (e.g. a park) that separates two drastically different land use zones

C.   **Typical Zoning Controls and Exceptions**

1.   Rezoning or amendment is a zoning change for an entire area

2.   Downzoning is a zoning change from dense to less dense usage

3.   Upzoning is a change from less dense to more dense usage

4.   Spot zoning is reclassification of a small area of land for use that does not conform to the zoning of the rest of the area

5.   Legal nonconforming use allows owner to continue present use that no longer complies with current zoning (also called grandfathering)

6. Setback, sideyard, and rearyard restrictions limit the location of improvements in relation to the position of the street

7. _Zoning law_
    <u>Variance</u> allows individual owner to vary or deviate to prevent economic hardship

8. Special (conditional) use (also called a special exception) is a specific type of variance allowing a different use

    a. No zoning change

    b. Buyers wishing to continue the use should make purchase agreement subject to obtaining special use permit

III. BUILDING CODES

A. Regulate building and construction standards

1. Designed to provide minimum standards

2. There are national and local standards – <u>strictest standard prevails</u>

B. Building inspectors are responsible for enforcing building codes

Can make an <u>exception</u> when safety isn't compromised and standards not specifically violated

After 540's the
Gov will take over
the property if don't
by and!

IV. ENVIRONMENTAL HAZARDS AND REGULATIONS

A. Lead-Based Paint

1. Agent must give copy of EPA pamphlet to buyers and tenants of homes built <u>before 1978</u>.

2. Buyers have 10-day opportunity to have home tested

3. Include warnings on purchase agreement and obtain signatures of buyers, sellers and agents.

B. Radon gas

1. An odorless radioactive gas that enters through cracks in the basement and can cause lung cancer

2. The U.S. Environmental Protection Agency (EPA) has determined what is an action level, but testing is not required

3. Measured in pico-curies per liter of air (pCi/L). <u>Measured using an alpha-track detector or electret ion chamber detector</u>

C. Asbestos

1. A material used for many years as insulation

2. Asbestos dust can be dangerous or even life threatening

D. Urea-formaldehyde foam insulation (UFFI)

1. A synthetic material pumped between the walls as insulation

2. It is dangerous because of gases released after it hardens.

E. **Groundwater contamination**

    1. Comes from several sources

    2. Most common are underground storage tanks, use of pesticides on farms, and waste disposal sites

F. **Environmental Impact Statement (EIS)**

    1. A report that assesses the probable impact on the environment of a proposed project

    2. Required of federal agencies in advance of major government actions (e.g. new highway or bridge construction)

G. **Superfund Law**

    1. Law involving liability for clean-up of sites affected by toxic materials

    2. <u>Anyone who touches the land can bear liability, even a tenant or a bank who gets property via foreclosure</u>

V. **SUBDIVISIONS**

A. **Subdivision Map Act** *more on the local level f/ the communit*

    1. Establishes procedures for filing a subdivision plan when property is divided into <u>2 or more</u> parcels

    2. Controls physical design aspects of a subdivision; ensures that areas devoted to public use, such as streets, will be properly improved initially.

        a. <u>Developer is responsible for providing for streets, sidewalks, sewers, etc.</u> (Off-site improvements)

        b. Municipality will be responsible for their ongoing maintenance and functioning

        c. A commercial acre is the remainder of an acre of newly subdivided land after the area devoted to streets, sidewalks, curbs, etc., has been deducted from the acre.

B. **Subdivision Lands Law**

1. Describes forms of ownership allowed in a subdivision of <u>5 or more</u> parcels

2. Designed to prevent fraud and misrepresentation in selling of subdivisions

3. Public report

    a. Developer files a notice of intention and applies for a report

    b. Real Estate Commissioner issues a preliminary report or a conditional report, then a final public report *[handwritten: Pink]* *[handwritten: Yellow]* *[handwritten: white]*

        i. A potential buyer can reserve a property based on the preliminary report, and can enter into a purchase agreement based on the conditional report

        ii. No sales can be completed until final report is issued

        iii. Buyer must sign receipt stating that they have received and read the final report

    c. The current report must be given to all serious buyers

C. **Other Subdivision Requirements**

1. An Environmental Impact Report (EIR) is required if project will have a significant effect on the environment

2. Alquist-Priolo Earthquake Fault Zoning Act regulates development in earthquake zones

3. Street Improvement Act of 1911 authorizes local governing bodies to order street improvements (off-site improvements) and pay through a bond issue and special assessment

    • Subdivider can use money for off-site improvements, but <u>NOT for purchase of land</u>

D. **Interstate Land Sales Full Disclosure Act (ILSFDA)**

    1.   Federal anti-fraud law regulating the marketing and sales of unimproved residential lots sold in interstate commerce

    2.   Anti-fraud provisions apply to subdivisions of 25 lots or more

    3.   Disclosure requirements (CA final report qualifies) apply to subdivisions of 100 lots or more

    4.   If all lots are <u>20 acres or larger</u>, or zoned industrial or commercial, subdivision is exempt from ILSFDA

VI. WATER RIGHTS

A. <u>**Riparian rights**</u>

Incidental to ownership of land abutting flowing water (stream, river, or <u>watercourse</u>)

B. <u>**Littoral rights**</u> *SD Bay, Mission Bay, Del Mar Lagoon*

Incidental to ownership of land abutting water that is not flowing (lake, ocean, or <u>sea arm</u>)

C. **Other Terms**

    1.   <u>Accretion</u> is gradual addition to land through natural causes

    2.   Erosion is gradual loss of land through natural causes

    3.   <u>Avulsion</u> is the sudden loss of land through natural causes

CONTRACTS
(Salesperson 12%/18 questions; Broker 12%/24 questions)

I.   **CONTRACT BASICS**

A.   **Definition of a Contract**

An agreement between two or more parties to do or not to do a specific thing

consent
Capacity
Consideration
Lawful
object!

B.   **Conditions of a Contract**

1.   A <u>valid</u> contract contains all essential elements

2.   A <u>voidable</u> contract appears to be valid, but one party may disaffirm because, for example, that party was subject to duress, undue influence, fraud or misrepresentation

a.   Contract is valid <u>until voided</u> by injured party

b.   In case of misrepresentation, injured party has <u>1 year</u> to void contract after discovery of misrepresentation

3.   A <u>void</u> contract is not enforceable due to failure to contain all essential elements

C.   **Enforceable vs. Unenforceable**

1.   In addition to being valid, void, or voidable, a contract can be enforceable or unenforceable

2.   A void contract is, by definition unenforceable. A voidable contract is enforceable only by the injured party

3.   Valid contracts meet all essential elements, but can be <u>unenforceable</u> by the courts (e.g. certain oral contracts, statute of limitations has expired, laches [not enforced in timely manner])

D. **Parties to a Transaction; -or versus -ee**

Offer	One making offer = Offeror	One receiving offer = Offeree	
Lease	Landlord = Lessor	Tenant = Lessee	
Option	Seller = Optionor	Buyer = Optionee	
Purchase Agreement	Seller = Vendor	Buyer = Vendee	
Contract for Deed	Seller = Vendor	Buyer = Vendee	
Mortgage	Lender = Mortgagee	Buyer = Mortgagor	
Deed of Trust	Buyer = Trustor	Lender = Beneficiary	3rd party = Trustee
Deed	Seller = Grantor	Buyer = Grantee	

oral is e/yrs
written is y/yrs

II.   **PERFORMANCE AND DISCHARGE OF OBLIGATIONS**

     A.   **Unilateral vs. Bilateral**

         1.   Unilateral: "Promise exchanged for performance"

         2.   Bilateral: "Promise exchanged for a promise"

     B.   **Executed vs. Executory**

         1.   Executed – duties completed by both parties; performed

         2.   Executory – 1 or both parties need to complete part of the contract; yet to be fully performed

     C.   **Assignment vs. Novation**

         1.   Assignment – transfers obligation but retains at least some liability (see "Leases" later in this section)

         2.   Novation – a <u>new contract</u> replacing an old one; transfers obligation and liability, e.g., assumption with release

     D.   **Amendments**

     Changes or modifications to a contract must be in writing and signed by all parties

E.   **Addenda**

Additional material attached to and made part of the initial agreement document

F.   **Statute of Limitations**

1.   2 years for oral contracts

2.   4 years for written contracts

3.   Doctrine of laches is used by courts to deny a claim because of undue delay in assertion

III.   **ESSENTIAL ELEMENTS OF A VALID CONTRACT**

A.   **Capacity/Competent Parties**

1.   18 is age of majority. A contract with a minor is <u>void</u>

2.   Emancipated minor (14 or over and married; in military service; by court order)

3.   Sane

B.   **Consent/Mutual Agreement/<u>"Meeting of the Minds"</u>/Offer and Acceptance**

1.   Offer and communication of acceptance before offer has been withdrawn

a.   Qualified acceptance or counteroffer is rejection

b.   <u>Death of offeror prior to communication of acceptance voids offer</u>

2.   No fraud or misrepresentation

a.   Misrepresentation = false information

b.   Fraud = Intent to deceive (actual fraud); Party relies on misinformation (constructive fraud)

      3.   Genuine and free assent (otherwise, contract can be <u>voidable</u>)

          a.   No undue influence

          b.   No duress (force, threat, unfair advantage)

C.   **Lawful Objective/Legal Purpose**

A contract for an illegal purpose is void

D.   **Consideration**

      1.   "Valuable" consideration refers to items or services of value

      2.   "Good" consideration is "love and affection"

      3.   "Sufficient" consideration is enough to be binding

      4.   "Adequate" consideration is fair market value – required to enforce specific performance

IV. STATUTE OF FRAUDS

A. Agreement in Writing

1. The <u>Statute of Frauds</u> requires that certain contracts be in writing to be enforceable

2. Includes contracts for the transfer of title to real estate, but NOT leases of 12 months or less.

3. Also includes debt agreements, commission agreements, and bills of sale for more than $500.

B. Agreement Signed

1. Certain agreements must be signed by the parties to be charged with the responsibility to perform

2. Both spouses must sign to sell community property or release homestead rights

V. TYPES OF REAL ESTATE CONTRACTS

A. Purchase Agreement/Offer to Purchase/Contract of Sale

1. Bilateral/Promise for a promise

2. Offer becomes a valid and binding contract when acceptance is communicated

3. Executory until performance by parties (closing)

4. Uniform Vendor and Purchaser Risk Act makes contract voidable by <u>buyer</u> if property is destroyed prior to closing, unless possession or title has passed

5. Death does not terminate contract

6. May include contingency clause allowing buyer to terminate under certain conditions

7. A 'time is of the essence' clause requires performance within the time specified

8. Earnest money is not required to create a valid purchase agreement

B. Option

1. Owner (optionor) sells right to purchase to prospective buyer (optionee) at a fixed price for a designated period

2. Option fee paid by optionee for the right

3. Optionor retains option fee if no performance by optionee

4. Unilateral contract; becomes bilateral when option exercised by optionee

C. Land Contract/Contract For Deed/Installment Contract/Real Property Sales Contract

1. Seller (vendor) retains legal title; buyer (vendee) has equitable title

2. Vendee takes possession when the contract is executed (if property is damaged or destroyed, vendee remains liable for payments)

3. Legal title transfers to buyer upon full performance

4. Death does not terminate contract

5. Vendor must use vendee's payments to satisfy obligations against the property

6. Contracts for deed cannot prohibit early payoff

D. **Listing Agreements (see Agency)**

E. **Lease**

    1.   Elements of a lease

        a.   Lessor and lessee names

        b.   Physical description of property *Address*

        c.   Rent terms *#—*

    2.   Lessor gives right to occupy to lessee and has <u>reversionary interest</u> to retake possession

    3.   Lessee may transfer rights

        a.   A <u>sublease</u> transfers <u>part</u> of the lessee's interest; original <u>lessee remains liable</u>

        b.   An <u>assignment</u> transfers the <u>entire</u> interest. Assignee is primarily liable, although assignor may have secondary liability without a novation

    4.   Types of leases

        a.   <u>Gross lease</u>/Fixed lease – Tenant pays fixed rent, landlord pays all expenses (utilities, taxes, special assessments) Lessor has burden of inflation under rent controls

        b.   <u>Net lease</u> – Tenant pays fixed rent plus expenses (utilities, taxes or special assessments). Most common for commercial property

        c.   <u>Percentage lease</u> – Retail tenant pays fixed rent plus % of <u>gross sales</u>

        d.   Land lease/<u>Ground lease</u> – Tenant rents unimproved property. Tenant improvements become the landlord's upon termination.

        e.   Graduated lease/Step-up lease – Rent increases or decreases at predetermined times and amounts

        f.   Sale-leaseback – Converts equity to capital without giving up possession

5. Constructive eviction – A tenant may vacate and be released of all further obligation if lessor does not meet obligations

6. A lease may be terminated by mutual agreement; this is called a <u>surrender</u>

VI. REMEDIES FOR BREACH OF CONTRACT / DEFAULT

A. Mutual Rescission

1. Mutual cancellation of obligations and return of all parties to their original condition before the contract was executed

2. Buyer may recover earnest money upon escrow officer receiving signed mutual release papers

B. Action for Damages

1. Suit for monetary damages

2. Accept liquidated damages

C. Specific Performance

- An action to force another party to buy or sell according to a contract

FINANCING
(Salesperson 13%/20 questions; Broker 13%/26 questions)

I.   **FINANCING INSTRUMENTS**

[handwritten: maur of the Note (receiver)]
[handwritten: Mortgage Note is negotiable]

A.   **Promissory Note**

1.   Evidence of a debt

2.   An unconditional promise signed by the maker (borrower) to pay a certain sum under set terms to the bearer/payee (lender)

3.   Secured by mortgage or trust deed

4.   A negotiable instrument considered personal property; cannot be recorded

5.   A "holder-in-due-course" receives the note in good faith ("innocent purchaser"); enjoys a favored position because maker cannot refuse to pay based on personal defenses; payee becomes the endorser

Sample Question:

[handwritten: 3927]

A seller takes back a note and second deed of trust for $11,220 and sells it immediately for $7,293. The amount of the discount on the note is most nearly:

   a. 28%
   b. 35%
   c. 54%
   d. 65%

[handwritten: 11,220 − 7,293 = 3,927]
[handwritten: 3,927 ÷ 11,220 = 35]

B.   **Mortgage and Deed of Trust**

NOTE: Mortgage and Trust Deed are often used synonymously. They are not the same, although they do have many elements in common.

1.   Security instruments that pledge (hypothecate) property as security for repayment without giving up possession

[handwritten left margin: Principle, Interest, Tax, Insurance]

2. Include covenants - causes of foreclosure

    a. Non-payment principal & interest

    b. Non-payment taxes

    c. Inadequate or no insurance

    d. Waste

3. Common Clauses

    a. <u>Alienation/Due on Sale clause</u> prevents assumption without lender's consent

    b. <u>Subordination clause</u> changes order/priority of liens

    c. <u>Acceleration clause</u> allows lender to demand immediate payment of entire balance owed if loan is in default

C. Mortgage

1. A mortgage is a 2-party instrument that conveys an interest in real property pledged as security for a debt.

2. Borrower = Mortgagor - Lender = Mortgagee

3. Most common financing instrument in U.S. California, however, favors Deeds of Trust

D. Deed of Trust/Trust Deed

1. 3-party instrument used instead of a mortgage

2. Borrower = Trustor; Lender = Beneficiary; 3rd party = Trustee

3. Property is conveyed by borrower to a third party (trustee) as security for loan

4. Trustee holds naked (bare legal) title on behalf of the lender (beneficiary)

5. Borrower (trustor) holds legal title and deed of trust is a lien

6. Trustee may sell the property in case of default

E. Satisfaction

1. When mortgage note is paid, mortgagee records satisfaction to release lien

2. When trust note is paid, trustee records <u>deed of reconveyance</u> to release lien (Do NOT confuse with a Trustee's Deed, which is used in the event of foreclosure)

F. Assumption Versus Subject To

1. If buyer purchases property "subject to" a mortgage, seller remains liable

- Buyer could still lose property and equity in the event of foreclosure, but would not be liable for any deficiency judgment

2. If buyer assumes, buyer becomes liable for the debt and lender releases original borrower's liability

3. There are no loan origination fees or points when borrower assumes or purchases subject to a mortgage

G. Land Contract/Real Property Sales Contracts/Installment Contract/ Contract for Deed

1. Form of owner financing and security arrangement

2. Seller (vendor) keeps legal title; buyer (vendee) has equitable title, takes possession and makes payments, receiving deed when payments are complete

3. Process used for Cal-Vet Loans, where Department of Veterans Affairs purchases property and sells to veteran under a land contract

4. Vendor <u>must</u> use payments from vendee to make any existing loan payments prior to using it for another purpose

II.   **FORECLOSURE**

Foreclosure is a legal procedure whereby property used as security for a debt is taken by a creditor or sold to pay off the debt.

A.   **Judicial Foreclosure/Equitable Action (for Mortgages)**

1.   Lawsuit brought by mortgagee in superior court to obtain court order to sell

2.   Property sold by sheriff to high bidder at public sale

3.   Borrower can stop foreclosure anytime prior to sale by paying past delinquencies, costs and fees (<u>Reinstatement</u> or redemption)

4.   If sale proceeds exceed cost of sale and foreclosing lien, excess goes to pay off junior liens in order of priority

5.   Certificate of sale is given to highest bidder, but borrower still has "statutory right of redemption". At end of redemption period, high bidder receives a Sheriff's Deed

6.   <u>Property owner (borrower) retains possession during foreclosure proceedings</u>

7.   If sale does not cover amount of loan, lender may file for a <u>deficiency judgment</u>. But no deficiency judgment can be obtained for purchase money loans used to finance owner-occupied home of 4 units or less

B. Non-Judicial Foreclosure (Trust Deeds)

1. No lawsuit necessary. Foreclosure is made by public sale

2. Requires 3 months Notification of Default. Within 10 days of recording the Notice of Default, a copy must be sent to trustor

3. Notice of Sale

   a. Trustor can stop the sale up to 5 business days prior to sale by curing deficiency and paying costs

   b. Notice of Sale must be published once a week (3 times) for 20 days. Notice must also be posted in public place (City Hall, courthouse, etc.)

4. Property sold to high bidder at a Trustee's Sale. Title transferred under a <u>Trustee's Deed</u>

5. No deficiency judgments are allowed on non-judicial foreclosures

C. Quiet Title Action (Cal-Vet Instrument)

1. A form of judicial foreclosure where the seller imposes a "quiet title action" in court

2. Buyer may have action for refund or redemption

D. Deed in Lieu of Foreclosure

1. Alternative to foreclosure – mortgagor/trustor deeds to mortgagee/beneficiary

2. Disadvantage to lender: it does not wipe out junior liens

III.   **METHODS OF DEBT REPAYMENT/DEBT SERVICE**

    A.   **Term (Straight)**

        1.   Interest only until maturity at end of term

        2.   Entire principal in one lump sum

    B.   **Fully <u>Amortized</u>**

        1.   Equal payments of principal & interest such that the balance becomes "0"

        2.   Payments at regular intervals

        3.   Interest is usually paid in arrears

    C.   **Partially Amortized/Balloon**

        1.   Equal payments of principal & interest

        2.   Balloon before end of term

    D.   **Graduated Payment**

        1.   Lower payments in beginning, payments increase, then level off

        2.   May have negative amortization (principal may increase)

    E.   **Adjustable Rate Mortgage (ARM)/Trust Deed**

        1.   Rate subject to change based upon changes in an economic index

        2.   May include interest and/or payment caps

F.   **Reverse Annuity Mortgage/Trust Deed**

     1.   Payments paid to mortgagor over specific term

     2.   Due upon sale of property, death of mortgagor(s), or at the end of the term

G.   **Shared Appreciation Mortgage/Trust Deed**

     Lender receives a portion of the profit when property is sold in return for lower interest rate

IV.   **TYPES OF TRUST DEEDS (AND MORTGAGES)**

A.   <u>**Package**</u>

     1.   Personal property is included as security in addition to real property

     2.   May be used to finance the purchase of a furnished condominium, etc.

B.   <u>**Blanket**</u>

     1.   More than one property pledged as security

     2.   A <u>release clause</u> allows a sub-divider to remove individual parcels as they are sold

        •   Releases are not done in equal amounts; i.e. first parcel released will usually be worth more

C.   **Open-End** *Home Equity line — up to '100,000.00 tax deductable*

     1.   Allows the borrower to obtain further advances at a later date

     2.   Future advance is limited to difference between original loan amount and current amount owed

D.   **Seller Carry-Back Purchase Money**

    1.   Owner financing where title transfers to buyer

    2.   Seller "takes back" a trust deed/mortgage as partial payment; seller has lien

No Gov loan

E.   **Conventional/Insured Conventional**

    1.   Debt repayment based solely on borrower's ability to pay; not insured or guaranteed by government

    2.   Depending on loan-to-value ratio, lender may require private mortgage insurance (PMI)

    3.   If required, PMI premium is paid to Mortgage Guarantee Insurance Corporation (MGIC)

F.   **Wraparound**

    1.   Junior financing that includes the remaining first loan balance which the buyer does NOT assume

    2.   Usually only used with seller financing

G.   **<u>Construction</u>**

    1.   <u>Interim</u> financing made available in installments as improvements are completed

    2.   Typically adjustable rate/short term from commercial banks

    3.   Lender may require a commitment for "take out"—a take-out loan replaces the construction loan with longer-term financing

V. MISCELLANEOUS MORTGAGE TERMS

A. Loan-to-Value Ratio/Mortgage Ratio

1. Maximum percentage of value lender will loan

2. Based on price or appraisal, whichever is less

B. Equity

1.
   Market value today
   - Total debt today
   Equity today

2. Leverage is the use of debt financing of an investment to maximize the return per dollar of equity invested

C. Points/Loan Origination Fee

1. Discount points are charged by the lender to increase lender's yield
   1 point = 1% of loan amount

2. Loan origination fee is charged by the lender to process and issue a loan

D. Other Clauses

1. A subordination clause allows a change in the order/priority of mortgages

2. An escalator clause allows the lender to increase the interest rate in the event of late payment or default

3. A lock-in-clause prohibits the early payoff of the loan

4. A prepayment penalty clause allows a borrower to pay off the loan early but lender can charge punitive interest

VI.   **SOURCES OF CAPITAL FOR REAL ESTATE LOANS**

   A.   **Commercial Banks**

   Prefer short-term loans for commercial, business, and new construction

   B.   **Savings and Loan Associations**

   Conventional, FHA and VA home loans

   C.   **Mortgage Bankers and Mortgage Brokers**

   1.   Mortgage brokers act as an intermediary between borrowers and lenders, but don't usually service loans

   2.   Mortgage bankers originate and service loans with deposits and their own money

   D.   **Life Insurance Companies/Credit Unions/Pension Funds**

   1.   Prefer long-term commercial and industrial participation loans

   2.   Lender receives interest plus an equity position in income-producing properties

VII. **GOVERNMENT PROGRAMS**

Funds come from qualified lenders approved by HUD

A. **FHA (Federal Housing Administration) Fully Insured Financing**

1. FHA <u>insures</u> lender against loss due to foreclosure

2. Enables high loan-to-value ratio

3. Mutual Mortgage Insurance (MMI) premiums may be paid at closing or financed

4. Property must meet <u>Minimum Property Requirements</u> (MPRs)

B. **VA (Veteran's Administration) Fully Guaranteed Financing**

1. <u>Guarantees</u> lenders against loss on loans to veterans

2. Can have up to 100% loan-to-value ratio

3. Two certificates required:

   a. Certificate of eligibility / entitlement

   b. Certificate of reasonable value (CRV) is VA appraisal

C. **Miscellaneous Aspects of FHA/VA**

1. Rules regarding assumption depend upon the date of the loan

2. No prepayment penalty

3. Non-veterans may assume VA loans

4. Purchase agreement must contain "escape clause," making sale contingent upon property being appraised at sales price or higher

D. **Cal-Vet (California Veterans Farm and Home Purchase Act)**

1. The Department of Veterans Affairs administers the program and is a <u>direct lender</u>

The leanter has the title till the End of the loan

2. The DVA purchases the property, then resells to veteran under a real property sales contract/land contract; veteran has equitable title; gets legal title when the loan is repaid

3. Veteran is required to acquire a life insurance policy which will pay off the loan in case of death

4. Also requires impound accounts (reserves) and cannot have a prepayment penalty

E. **The Federal Reserve Bank (The "Fed")**

1. The nation's central bank, charged with regulating the nation's money supply

2. Regulates rate of growth/inflation by:

   a. Authorizing the printing of more money

      i. Too much money in system creates inflation

      ii. Too little money can cause recession

*curraney
Reserve Feld
Discount Rate
Buying Selly Bonds*

   b. Regulating reserve requirements of banks

      i. Increases reserve requirements to "stem" (slow) inflation/slow economic growth

      ii. Decreases reserve requirements to stimulate economic growth

   c. Setting the "discount rate" – interest charged to member banks

      i. Raises rate to stem inflation/slow growth

      ii. Lowers rate to stimulate growth

Fed Funds Rate

d.   Buying or selling government bonds

    i.   Buying bonds, banks receive influx of cash to make more loans – stimulates growth

    ii.   Selling bonds takes money from the economy – slows growth

F.   Secondary Mortgage Market

1.   Where loans are bought and sold; NOT originated

2.   Organizations that sell mortgage-backed securities to investors:

    a.   FNMA buys all types of mortgages (Federal National Mortgage Association - "Fannie Mae")

    b.   GNMA buys FHA/VA mortgages (Government National Mortgage Association - "Ginnie Mae") *still Gov agency*

    c.   FHLMC buys from S&L's and commercial banks (Federal Home Loan Mortgage Corp. - "Freddie Mac")

3.   To verify the loan balance upon purchasing the mortgage, investor or secondary market purchaser will ask for a <u>beneficiary statement</u> or estoppel certificate

4.   When a loan is sold for less than its face amount, it's called <u>discounting</u>

FINANCING/CREDIT LAWS

A.   **Regulation Z / Truth-in-Lending – Federal Reserve Board Regulates**

    1.   <u>Purpose</u>: Promote the informed use of consumer credit by requiring meaningful disclosures about its terms and cost.

    2.   Applies only to loans from institutional lenders to consumers for personal, family, or household purposes

    3.   Does not apply to loans for business, commercial (construction loans, building with 5+ units) or agricultural purposes, nor to credit over $25,000 if it's not secured by principal residence

    4.   Disclosure/advertising requirements

        a.   <u>Annual percentage rate</u> (APR) is the effective rate that includes the <u>nominal interest rate</u> (the rate listed in loan documents/promissory note) <u>plus finance charges</u> (loan origination fees, interest, discount points, and assumption fees)

        b.   Price and/or APR are the only specific finance terms allowed in ads without triggering full disclosure; General terms are okay ("low interest")

        c.   If the nominal interest rate, down payment, monthly payment, or number of payments is mentioned in ad, this triggers full disclosure

        d.   Full disclosure includes APR, down payment, finance charges and terms of repayment (monthly payments, number of payments, etc.)

5.   Customer has a limited right to rescind a credit transaction

      a.   Must be a junior loan or refinancing loan when principal residence is used as security

      b.   Borrower has until midnight of 3rd business day after consummation of the contract or delivery of disclosure statement, whichever is later

      c.   Does not apply to seller financing

B.   RESPA – Real Estate Settlement Procedures Act

1.   Standardizes closing practices for certain transactions

      a.   Applies to 1st mortgages or trust deeds, purchase money loans made by federally regulated or insured lenders for loans secured by 1-4, owner-occupied residences

      b.   Does not apply to home improvement or construction loans, vacant lots, loan assumptions, parcels of 25 acres or more, or land sales contracts

2.   Restricts amount of advance escrow payments for taxes and insurance

3.   Lender must give Guide to Settlement Costs booklet and good faith estimate of all closing costs at time of application or within 3 business days

4.   Borrower has right to inspect Uniform Settlement Statement (HUD-1) 1 day before closing. Statement must be delivered at or before closing

      a.   If borrower waives right of delivery, the Uniform Settlement Statement must be mailed as soon as practicable after settlement

      b.   Lenders may NOT charge a fee for preparing the statement

5.   Prohibits "kickbacks" for unearned fees, such as lenders, insurance agencies, escrow companies, or home protection companies paying money for referrals by brokers

IX. **LOAN BROKERAGE**

A. **Broker definition (Article 1)**

A person who sells, exchanges or acquires 8 or more real estate notes or sales contracts with the public in a calendar year

B. **The broker shall cause the security instrument (mortgage or trust deed) to be recorded or recommend such recording (Article 5)**

C. **Mortgage Loan Disclosure Statement**

1. Disclosure required for all loans negotiated by licensees for 1-4 family residential transactions

2. Must be signed by both borrower and licensee and delivered to borrower before he or she becomes obligated

3. Broker lending his or her own funds must disclose this fact

D. **Limits on loan brokerage commissions**

1. Article 7 limits the commission and fees brokers can charge for brokering loans: the limitations ONLY apply to first loans of less than $30,000 or secondary loans of less than $20,000. The limits are as follows:

a. For first loans, maximum 5% commission if loan is less than 3 years; 10% if more than 3 years.

b. For junior loans, maximum 5% if loan is less than 2 years; 10% if it's between 2 years and 3 years; 15% if more than 3 years.

LAW OF AGENCY
(Salesperson 12%/18 questions;
Broker 12%/24 questions)

I.   **PARTIES TO AN AGENCY RELATIONSHIP**

    A.   **Principal**

       1.   One who employs another to act on his behalf

       2.   Consumer principal is a "client"

    B.   **Agent/Fiduciary**

       1.   One who is employed to represent a principal

       2.   Fiduciary is the highest trust relationship under law – must put the client's interest above one's own

    C.   **Subagent**

       1.   One to whom an agent has delegated agency powers

       2.   If you show another company's listing to a buyer you do not represent, you are likely acting as a subagent; a subagent usually <u>represents the seller</u>

    D.   **Third Party**

       1.   A party to a transaction who is not a party to the particular agency agreement

       2.   Consumer third party buyer is a "customer"

II.   **TYPES OF AGENCY AND CREATION OF AGENCY**

A.   **Types of Agency**

    1.   Special agency is created when an agent is authorized to perform a particular act without the ability to bind the principal

        a.   Seller contracts with a broker

        b.   Buyer contracts with a broker

    2.   General agency is created when an agent is authorized to perform a series of acts associated with the continued operation of a particular business

        a.   Salesperson licensed to a broker

        b.   Property manager employed by a property owner

    3.   An <u>attorney-in-fact</u> is authorized to perform in place of the principal. This is accomplished through a power of attorney

B.   **Creation of Agency**

    1.   Express agency is created through an oral or written agreement

    2.   Implied agency is created through the actions of the parties

    3.   Agency by ratification is created "after the fact," when a previously unauthorized action is confirmed by a principal

    4.   Ostensible agency or <u>agency by estoppel</u> is created when a third party is led to believe an agency relationship exists

    5.   Compensation is <u>not</u> a requirement of an agency relationship. Who pays the agent does not determine whom the agent represents

III. RESPONSIBILITIES OF AGENT/DISCLOSURE OF AGENCY

    A.   An agent owes a principal/client <u>fiduciary</u> obligations (OLD CAR)

        1.   Obedience

            a.   Must obey lawful instructions of client

            b.   If prior to listing, a potential client asks broker to do something illegal, broker should decline listing

        2.   Loyalty

        3.   Disclosure *, Elect, confirm*

        4.   Confidentiality

        5.   Accounting

        6.   Reasonable Care and Skill

    B.   Disclosure of Representation

        1.   Disclose representation as soon as practical

        2.   Agency disclosure form must be provided and signed before signing of listing or writing of offer

        3.   Confirmation of agency relationships is required before entering into a contract (<u>Process is: Disclosure, election, confirmation</u>)

        4.   Must disclose if representing or <u>working with a relative</u> or any person with whom agent has significant relationship (e.g. best friend, etc.)

        5.   If representation changes, a new disclosure is required <u>at once</u>

        6.   When representing both the buyer and the seller (dual agency), agent must get consent of both parties in writing – <u>undisclosed dual agency, also called divided agency, is illegal</u>

7.   Broker owes those they don't represent honesty and fair dealing, <u>even if principal asks to lie or keep silent</u>

C.   Transfer Disclosure Statement (TDS)

1.   Required of both seller and agent with exceptions, which include foreclosures, co-owner to co-owner sales, or other examples where seller would not have knowledge of the property or would not need disclosure

2.   <u>Easton vs. Strassburger</u> decision requires licensees to disclose what they know and what they <u>should know</u>

a.   Requires licensee to conduct a visual inspection of accessible areas

b.   Does not need to inspect common areas of a condominium

D.   Additional Disclosures/Obligations

(Note: See Practice and Mandated Disclosure Section for further discussion of disclosures)

1.   Full fiduciary obligation of disclosure to client

2.   Disclosure of material facts to customer

a.   If death occurred on property within previous 3 years, must disclose cause (accident, murder, suicide, natural causes) but no details

b.   Agent has no duty to disclose death or affliction related to AIDS

3.   Must present all offers – multiple offers should be presented at the same time

4.   Listing agreements generally authorize broker to collect earnest money deposits along with offers. If not authorized to do so, broker can accept deposits, but becomes an agent of the buyer for that deposit

5. Earnest money/deposits

    a. Must disclose to seller the form of deposit taken with an offer

    b. Promissory notes/post-dated checks may be taken, but facts MUST be fully disclosed

    c. Money should be deposited in trust account or into escrow by end of 3rd business day following receipt, unless the offeror instructs the agent not to deposit the money until after offer is accepted, and seller is informed of this fact

6. Must disclose that commissions are negotiable in listing agreement

E.   **Liability for Another's Acts**

1. Each broker is responsible for the professional actions of the salespeople he or she sponsors

2. A principal is responsible for misrepresentations made by his or her agent within the scope of their authority

F.   **Multiple listing service (MLS)**

1. Widely used arrangement by which brokers pool listings and offer "cooperation" to other brokers

2. Cooperating brokers must obey all the laws of agency

IV.   **THE LISTING AGREEMENT**

A personal service contract/employment contract between a broker and a seller that establishes an agency relationship and grants broker the authority to seek buyers and obtain offers.

A.   **Types of Listings**

1. Exclusive right to sell

    a. Agent is paid regardless of who obtains the buyer

    b. Gives maximum broker protection by eliminating procuring cause disagreements

2.   Exclusive agency

    a.   Owner retains right to sell himself without paying a commission

    b.   If anyone other than the owner obtains the buyer, agent gets paid

Have a Termination Date !

3.   Open/non-exclusive

    a.   Owner may list with more than one broker

    b.   Listing broker is paid only if he obtains buyer, causing possible procuring cause disagreements

    c.   May be terminated at any time prior to performance

4.   Net listing

    a.   Broker receives as commission all money above a minimum guaranteed sales price

    b.   Legal but discouraged in California; broker must reveal amount of expected commission before seller enters into purchase contract

5.   Option Listing

    a.   Used when the broker may want to purchase the property

    b.   Broker must reveal expected profit

B.   Essential Elements of a Listing

1.   In writing and signed by the owner in order to be enforceable

2.   Amount/method of compensation paid to the <u>listing broker</u> is negotiable.

3.   Price and terms

4.   <u>Definite</u> beginning and <u>termination date</u> for exclusive listings

5.   Agent's authority

C.   **How a Listing Terminates**

    1.   Performance by both parties (<u>completion</u> of the sale)

    2.   Expiration of term

    3.   Revocation by principal/Renunciation by broker/Mutual Rescission

    4.   Death or incapacity of either broker or seller (NOTE: death of salesperson does NOT terminate a listing). <u>Listings belong to the broker</u>

    5.   Destruction of premises

    6.   Bankruptcy of either broker or seller

D.   **Safety Clause/Broker Protection Clause/Extender Clause**

    1.   A clause that provides for a broker to collect a commission for a certain length of time after the termination of the listing, if a buyer the broker procured during the listing purchases the property

    2.   Broker usually required to submit names <u>in writing</u> of potential buyers to whom property has been shown prior to listing termination

E.   **When Commissions Are Earned**

    1.   When broker procures ready, willing and able buyer, or

    2.   When seller accepts an offer presented by a broker

V.   BUYER AGENCY AGREEMENT

 A.   Types of Buyer Representation Agreements

  1. Exclusive right to represent authorizes one broker to represent the buyer and requires buyer to compensate agent when purchasing property through any source.

  2. Non-exclusive (open) right to represent allows the buyer to work with any broker but owes compensation only if the buyer uses the broker's services

 B.   Termination of Buyer Representation Agreements

  Same as listing agreements (death, bankruptcy, etc.). Buyer Representation Agreements must have definite termination date

VI.   BROKER/SALESPERSON RELATIONSHIPS

 A.   Employment Contract

  1. Regulations of the Real Estate Commissioner require brokers to have written agreements with a salesperson

  2. Under real estate law, salespeople are employees of the broker, even if contract defines them as independent contractors for tax purposes

 B.   Internal Revenue Service

  1. IRS may classify a salesperson as an employee or an independent contractor

  2. Employees are under direct control of employers; can be told how to perform job

  3. Independent contractors are compensated based on results; employers have less control over how job is done

PRACTICE OF REAL ESTATE AND MANDATED DISCLOSURES
(Salesperson 24%/36 questions; Broker 27%/54 questions)

I.   **FAIR HOUSING**

A.   **Civil Rights Act of 1866**

The Civil Rights Act of 1866 prohibits discrimination based upon an individual's race or ancestry

B.   **Federal Fair Housing – Protected Classifications**

1.   Race (only protected class in the 1866 Civil Rights Act)

2.   Religion

3.   Color

4.   National Origin

5.   Sex (added in 1974)

6.   Family Status (added in 1988)

7.   Handicap/Disability (added in 1988)

C.   **California Fair Housing Laws**

1.   California Fair Housing Laws include The Unruh Civil Rights Act and the Fair Employment and Housing Act (Rumford Act), the Housing Financial Discrimination Act (Holden Act)

2.   Stricter than federal acts; include age and marital status as protected classifications

D. **Prohibited Actions**

1. Less favorable treatment (including refusal to show property)

2. Discriminatory or restrictive advertising

3. <u>Steering</u> – the channeling of potential buyers to or away from particular areas as a means of discrimination

4. <u>Blockbusting</u> – also called <u>panic peddling</u>, inducing people to sell their homes because of the entry into the neighborhood of members of protected classes

5. Redlining – refusing to offer or limiting loans in certain areas

E. **Exceptions to Federal Fair Housing Act**

<u>There are NO exceptions in regard to racial discrimination</u>. It is not a violation to discriminate against other protected classifications in the following situations:

1. Rental or sale of a single-family home (no broker involvement and no discriminatory advertising)

2. Rental of units (4-unit building or less) where the owner occupies one of the units (no broker involvement and no discriminatory advertising)

3. Units owned by religious organizations may be restricted to people of the same religion if membership in the organization is not restricted on the basis of race, color, or national origin

4. Non-profit organizations may restrict to members only

5. Rental of units based on familial status involving buildings with at least 80% of occupants 55+

F. **HUD Equal Housing Opportunity Poster**

    1.   Must be prominently displayed in broker's office

    2.   Failure to display can be considered evidence of discrimination and, if there is a complaint, shift burden of proof to broker

G. **Americans with Disabilities Act (ADA)**

    1.   Ensures equal <u>access</u> to public accommodations for disabled persons

    2.   Requires removal of architectural and communication barriers when "readily achievable"

    3.   Allows disabled tenants to make changes at their expense – owner may require tenant to return property to original condition upon termination of lease

    4.   Also prohibits employment discrimination against the disabled if 15+ employees

II. **TRUST ACCOUNTS AND RECORD KEEPING**

A. **Trust Accounts**

up to $200

    1.   The purpose of trust fund accounting is to keep a broker's funds separate from those of the broker's clients

    2.   <u>Commingling</u> of trust funds with funds belonging to the licensee is prohibited; the actual use of trust funds for purposes other than their intended purpose is conversion and is a felony

    3.   Most common trust fund handling comes with accepting earnest money deposits (see Agency)

4.   Trust funds can be withdrawn only with the signature of the following:

      a.   The broker in whose name the account is maintained

      b.   Designated broker-officer if account is in the name of a corporate broker

      c.   If specifically authorized in writing, a salesperson sponsored by the broker

      d.   If specifically authorized in writing, an unlicensed employee of the broker covered by a fidelity bond at least equal to the maximum amount to which the person has access

B.   Record Keeping

1.   Broker is responsible for maintaining adequate records

2.   Broker must <u>reconcile</u> the trust accounts on a <u>monthly basis</u> to check that the money in the account is equal to its liability

3.   Trust fund records must be kept for 3 years, and must be open for inspection by the Real Estate Commissioner

III.   LICENSING AND CONTINUING EDUCATION REQUIREMENTS

A.   A Real Estate License is required for:

1.   Selling or offering to sell property or negotiate for the sale or purchase of property for another for a fee; <u>soliciting</u> prospective buyers and sellers

2.   Selling of used (registered) mobile homes

3.   Acting as a mortgage loan broker

4.   Buying, selling, or exchanging, or offering to buy sell or exchange real property sales contracts or promissory notes secured by real property liens (real estate paper) for another for a fee

5.   As a principal, buying, selling, or exchanging 8 or more real property sales contracts or promissory notes secured by real property (real estate paper) in one calendar year

B.   A Real Estate License is NOT required for:

1.   Buying or selling one's own property (unless one is in the business)

2.   A corporation dealing with its own property

3.   An attorney when performing duties as an attorney-at-law

4.   A person acting as an attorney-in-fact under power of attorney from the owner

5.   A person acting under order of court (e.g. executor of a will)

6.   An assistant provided that person does not quote or discuss price or terms or otherwise perform duties requiring a license (NO SOLICITATION); escrow officers

C.   Initial Salesperson Licensing Requirements

1.   18 years old

2.   Completion of a college-level course in Real Estate Principles

3.   Passing Licensing Examination

4.   Application for a license within <u>1 year of exam date</u>

5.   Proof of legal presence

6.   Applicants may not earn commissions until license is physically received

D. Additional Salesperson Licensing Requirements

1. An initial license is valid for 4 years, but...

2. It is a Conditional License for up to <u>18 months</u>, until a licensee takes 2 additional college-level courses

3. For the 1st renewal, a licensee must also take 12 hours in <u>Agency, Ethics, Trust Fund Handling and Fair Housing</u>

4. For each successive renewal, licensee must complete 45 hours of continuing education, including 6 hours in Agency, Ethics, Trust Fund Handling, and Fair Housing

E. Broker Licensing Requirements

1. Eight college level courses

2. 2 years experience in a real estate related profession, or 1 year plus a 2-year college degree, or a 4-year college degree

F. Acting Without a License

1. Performing activities that require a license without a license subjects person to a <u>$10,000</u> fine and/or 6 months in jail. Corporations are subject o $50,000 fine

2. Licensee would also be subject to a fine of $100 for employing or compensating an unlicensed person to perform acts requiring a license

IV.   **DRE JURISDICTION AND DISCIPLINARY ACTIONS**

    A.   **Composition and Powers of the Department of Real Estate (DRE)**

        1.   The DRE is a department within the Business, Transportation and Housing Agency and is headed by the Real Estate Commissioner

        2.   The Real Estate Commissioner is appointed by the Governor

        3.   Powers of the DRE include:

            a.   Promulgating policies on the enforcement of real estate law

            b.   Regulating licensees and enforcing real estate law

            c.   Regulating new subdivisions

        4.   The DRE does NOT mediate commission disputes or collect penalties from victims of licensees

    B.   **Violations of the Real Estate Law – Examples of Unlawful Conduct**

        1.   Knowingly misrepresenting value of property to get a listing or secure a buyer

        2.   Representing to an owner when seeking a listing that the licensee has obtained a written offer when licensee has no such written offer

        3.   Stating or implying that the licensee is prohibited by law or regulation from charging less than the quoted commission

        4.   Misrepresenting the licensee's relationship with a broker or the broker's responsibility for acts of the licensee

        5.   Knowingly underestimating closing costs

        6.   Knowing making a false or misleading representation regarding the form, amount, and/or treatment of an earnest money deposit

7. Knowing making a false or misleading representation to a seller financing part of a sale regarding buyer's ability to pay

8. Making an addition or modification to the terms of an agreement previously signed by a party without the knowledge and consent of the party

9. When acting as a principal for real estate paper, making a representation regarding the value of securing property without reasonable basis for believing it is accurate

10. Making a representation regarding the nature and/or condition of the features of a property, the size or boundaries of the property, or the legal use of the property without having a reasonable basis for believing it to be true

11. When acting as an agent, failing to disclose to a prospective purchaser material facts about the property

12. When acting as a listing agent, failing to present any written offer unless instructed by the owner not to present such an offer

13. When acting as a listing agent, presenting competing offers in a manner that would induce the owner to accept an offer that provides greater compensation to the agent

14. Failing to explain to the prospective parties for whom the licensee is acting as an agent the meaning and probable significance of a contingency in an offer or contract that may affect the closing date

15. Failing to disclose to a seller whom the licensee represents the nature and extent of any direct or indirect interest that the licensee expects to acquire as a result of the sale. Also must disclose if a relative or person with whom licensee has a special relationship may be acquiring an interest. Same rule applies to representing a buyer and having an interest in the property buyer may acquire.

16. Failing to disclose to a principal any significant interest the licensee has in an entity the agent recommends

17. When acting as an agent for the seller, refunding any part of an offeror's deposit after the seller has accepted the offer, unless the licensee has express permission from the seller to make the refund

V. CALIFORNIA REAL ESTATE RECOVERY FUND

A. Purpose

1. Portions of license fees are placed into an account from which members of the public can be compensated for illegal acts of licensees

2. Funds can be disbursed if a judgment has been obtained and the debt is uncollectible from the licensee

3. The license is suspended until the licensee makes payment back to the fund

B. Limits

1. $20,000 limit per transaction

2. $100,000 limit against one licensee

VI. TRUTH IN ADVERTISING

A. False advertising is grounds for revocation or suspension of a license

B. Blind advertising

1. Blind advertising does not list the name of an agent where an agent is involved

2. All advertising of an activity for which a license is required must indicate a licensee designation ("agent" would meet the requirement)

VII.   MANDATED DISCLOSURES

A.   Transfer Disclosure Statement (TDS)

1.   Seller and agent must provide a TDS for sales of 1-4 unit residential property as soon as practicable before transfer

2.   Transactions, such as foreclosures, where seller would not know condition of property are exempted

3.   Buyer's right to rescind

    a.   Buyer has 3 days to terminate contract after TDS is personally delivered

    b.   Buyer has 5 days to terminate contract after TDS is mailed

    c.   If changes are made to the TDS, the buyer again has <u>right to rescind</u>

B.   Natural Hazards Disclosure Form – Sellers and Agents must sign

1.   Earthquake Disclosures

    a.   When selling 1-4 unit residential property built prior to <u>January 1, 1960</u>, seller must disclose whether dwelling has earthquake weaknesses

    b.   For all residences, earthquake safety disclosure ("Residential Earthquake Hazard Report") must be filled out and signed by buyer and seller

    b.   Alquist-Priolo Earthquake Fault Zone Act requires disclosure if property is located within a geologic hazard zone

    c.   Seismic Hazard Mapping Act

2.   Dam Failure Inundation

3.   Very High Fire Hazard Zone

4.   Wildfire Risk Areas

5.   100 Year Flood Zones

C. **Environmental Hazards Pamphlet**

1. In addition to disclosing environmental (as opposed to natural) hazards in the TDS, sellers and agents can provide a prepared pamphlet

2. If pamphlet is provided, neither seller nor agent has a duty to provide further information regarding environmental hazards (except for lead-based paint disclosure) unless there is actual knowledge

D. **Mello-Roos Disclosure**

<u>Seller</u> of 1-4 unit dwelling must disclose if property is subject to a Mello-Roos lien

E. **Seller Financing Disclosure**

If there is seller financing, the "Seller Financing Addendum and Disclosure" is required

F. **Other Required Disclosures**

1. Megan's Law – all purchase contracts must include a notice informing buyers or lessees of the public availability of information regarding registered sex-offenders

2. Home Energy Ratings

3. Home Inspection Notice – for FHA financing or HUD-owned property, borrower must sign notice, "Importance of a Home Inspection"

4. Smoke Detector Notice   P/Bedroom   P/Hallway

5. Water Heater Bracing

VIII.   PROPERTY MANAGEMENT/LANDLORD-TENANT

A.   License Requirement

1. A real estate license is required for property managers who rent, lease, solicit listings of places for rent, solicits for prospective tenants, collects rents, etc.

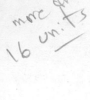

more than 16 units

2. A license is not required for a resident manager, if his or her management activities are confined to the complex in which the manager lives

B.   Security Deposits

Amount of security deposits that can be collected <u>depends on</u>:

2 months F/ unfurnished
3 months F/ furnished

a. Term of lease

b. Whether apartment is furnished or unfurnished

C.   Landlord Warrants

1. Warrant of quiet enjoyment – lease will not be disturbed by someone claiming paramount title

2. Warrant of habitability – landlord must keep property in livable condition

3. If these are violated, tenant may have right of <u>constructive eviction</u>

D.   Unlawful detainer

1. A court action by a lessor to regain possession (eviction)

2. Notice to Quit required

IX. MISCELLANEOUS TERMS

A. Design and Construction

1. Flashing – metal used on roof to protect against water seepage

2. Mud sill – treated member bolted to foundation

3. Studs – vertical framework paced wall supports

4. Joists – parallel wooden beams that support flooring or ceiling loads

5. Footing – the base of a building on which the foundation is placed

6. BTU (British Thermal Unit) – unit of heat, used in rating a furnace or other heating unit

7. EER – Energy Efficiency Rating – the higher the rating, the more efficient the equipment

8. R-Value – measure of the effectiveness of insulation

9. Backfill – soil replaced against a foundation

10. Turnkey project – one in which the builder provides a completed facility ready for move-in

11.   Plans

     a.   Elevation Plan – shows the exterior sides of a structure after all construction has been completed

     b.   Floor Plan – Scale drawing showing all dimensions and placements of doors, windows, partitions, and built-ins

     c.   <u>Foundation Plan</u> – Scale drawing showing the dimensions of footings, piers, and details of subflooring

     d.   Plot Plan – Indicates lot dimensions and improvements draw to scale in proportion to the boundary lines. Also shows walks, driveways, and roof plan

B.   Measurements

1.   <u>Board foot</u> – 12" by 12" by 1' = 144 cubic inches. <u>Any 3 measurements</u> making up 144 cubic inches equals 1 board foot

2.   Square foot – Square yard conversion

     a.   A square foot is 1 foot by 1 foot

     b.   A square yard is 3 feet by 3 feet or 9 square feet

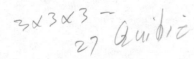

VALUATION AND MARKET ANALYSIS
(Salesperson 12% / 18 questions,
Broker 11% / 17 questions)

I. **VALUE**

An appraisal is <u>an estimate or opinion of market value</u> supported by an analysis of relevant property data.

A. **Market Value**

Market value is the highest price in terms of cash or its equivalent that a property will bring when:

1. a willing seller would sell and a willing buyer would buy,

2. the property is exposed for a reasonable time,

3. both parties are familiar with the property's uses, and

4. neither is under abnormal pressure to sell or buy.

B. **Market Price**

The actual price paid in a transaction. Price may deviate from value.

C. **Essential Elements of Value (DUST) – Cost is NOT an element of value**

1. Demand

2. Utility (usefulness)

3. Scarcity

4. Transferability

D.   Forces Influencing Value

1.   Physical

2.   Economic

3.   Social

4.   Governmental

E.   Subjective vs. Objective Value

1.   Subjective value – value-in-use

2.   Objective value – value-in-exchange (market value)

F.   Principles of Value

1.   Highest and best use

a.   Produces greatest net return on the land over time

b.   Not necessarily present use of the land

c.   Must be financially feasible, legally permitted, and considerate of adjacent land uses

2.   Principle of Substitution

a.   Value is determined by cost of acquiring an equally desirable substitute

b.   Principle of substitution is used in all three approaches to estimating value

3.   Supply and demand

    a.   Supply – amount of properties available. Prices move <u>opposite</u> supply. Large quantity for sale, prices go down.

    b.   Demand – amount of properties that will be purchased. Prices move <u>with</u> demand. If scarce and desired, prices go up.

4.   Anticipation – Value can increase or decrease due to some future benefit or detriment that will affect the property

5.   Conformity

    a.   Maximum value is reached if land use conforms to existing neighborhood standards

    b.   Neighborhood life cycle can be expressed in multiple ways:

        i.   Development/Stability/Decline/Re-development

        ii.   Integration/Equilibrium/Disintegration/Re-development

6.   Regression – value of over-improved property declines

7.   Progression – value of under-improved property increases

8.   Plottage – the increased value resulting from <u>assemblage</u>, combining adjacent lots into one larger lot

9.   Balance – point of maximum productivity and maximum value is achieved when all factors of production (land, labor, capital, coordination) are in balance

10.   Contribution – The value of an improvement depends upon how much it adds or detracts from the overall value

    a.   <u>Economic life</u> is period during which site improvements contribute to value

    b.   <u>Effective age</u> is based upon property's physical condition and usefulness

    c.   Chronological age is the actual age of the property

II.   **METHODS OF ESTIMATING VALUE/APPRAISAL PROCESS**

A.   **Sales Comparison Approach/Market Approach/Market Data Approach–
      Primarily Residential**

1.   Property evaluating - "subject"

2.   Similar properties recently sold — "comparables" or "comps"

3.   Adjustments are made to comparables

4.   Comp better "-"   Comp worse "+"

5.   <u>Competitive market analysis</u> (CMA) uses similar approach, but is not an appraisal

6.   Whenever possible, property is evaluated using comparison with recent sales

B.   **Cost Approach/Replacement Cost Approach – Most Effective Method for
      Special Purpose Buildings or New Construction**

1.   Estimate new construction cost

a.   Reproduction cost new – exact replica

b.   Replacement cost new - same function or utility

c.   Methods of estimating cost of new construction

i.   <u>Quantity survey</u> – a highly involved process of estimating cost of new construction by detailing raw material and installation costs; most difficult but most accurate method

ii.   Unit-Cost-in-Place Method estimates the installed price of components

iii.   Cubic Foot or Square Foot method estimates cost based on the dimensions of the property

2.   Subtract accrued depreciation (loss in value to the <u>building</u>)

     a.   Physical deterioration (wear and tear; deferred maintenance); can be curable (correctable at an economically feasible cost) or incurable

     b.   Functional obsolescence (e.g. inadequate design or equipment, over-improvement, improper improvement); can be curable or incurable

     c.   Economic/locational obsolescence (external force); always incurable

3.   Estimate land value (using market approach)

C.   Income Approach – Income-Producing Properties

1.   Capitalization

     a.   Conversion of future income to present value

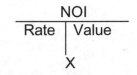

     b.   Income = Rate x (times) Value
             I = net annual income, R = cap rate, V = value

     c.   Net operating income (NOI) is determined as follows:

          i.   Annual/Potential Gross Income minus <u>vacancy</u> and credit loss equals Effective Gross Income (EGI)

          ii.   EGI minus operating expenses equals Net Operating Income

          iii.   Operating expenses include management costs, taxes, insurance, etc.

             •   Principal and Interest are not included.

             •   Management costs <u>are included</u> even if owner manages property or if a tenant manages in exchange for free rent

     d.   Investors will accept a <u>lower</u> cap rate for investments that are <u>less risky</u>; demand higher cap rate for projects that are riskier

2.   Gross rent multiplier (alternative to capitalization that takes into account <u>gross income</u> but not expenses)

Formulas:

Annual Gross Rent Multiplier × Annual Gross Rent = Value
OR
Monthly Gross Rent Multiplier x Monthly Gross Rent = Value

Sample Question:

Two investors were interested in purchasing property that had net incomes of $30,000. One investor used a capitalization rate of 5% and the other used a capitalization rate of 6%. What is the difference in values of these properties?

a. $45,000
b. $60,000
c. $100,000
d. $120,000

$$V = \frac{NOI}{CAP\ RAT}$$

D.   Additional Techniques/Variations

1.   Development Method

a.   Used to value undeveloped land by estimating its selling price as if it had been developed and then subtracting the cost to develop the site

b.   Sales/market approach is preferable method of estimating value of vacant land

2.   Property Residual Technique is used in the income approach to estimate the total value of the property, including land and improvements

a.   Land Residual Technique estimates the value of the land

d.   Building Residual Technique estimates the value of improvements

E.   Frontage/Front foot/4-3-2-1 rule

1.   <u>Frontage</u> is the length of property abutting a street

2.   Front foot is a measure of frontage used in appraising value of commercial property; each front foot is presumed to extend the depth of the lot

3.   4-3-2-1 Rule for Commercial Property

a.   40% of value exists in 1st 25% of property depth

b.   As depth decreases, overall value decreases and value per front foot decreases but value per square foot increases

F.   **Reconciliation Process**

1.   Final step in valuation process: Appraiser analyzes and weights estimates of value from market, cost and income approach

2.   Arrives at final estimate of value; NOT an average of the value estimates

G.   **A narrative report is the most comprehensive type of appraisal report**

III.   **THE FEDERAL INSTITUTIONS REFORM RECOVERY AND ENFORCEMENT ACT (FIRREA)**

A.   **Appraisers must comply with Uniform Standards of Professional Appraisal Practice (USPAP)**

B.   **Appraisals for federally-related loans must be performed by state-certified or licensed appraisers**

Federally related transactions include all loans made by federally chartered banks and savings and loans, and therefore include most residential loans

C.   **California Licensing Requirements**

1.   An appraiser with a residential license may appraise residential property (1-4 units) up to a transaction value of $1 million

2.   An appraiser who is a certified residential appraiser may appraise all residential property, and nonresidential property up to a transaction value of $250,000

3.   An appraiser who is a certified general appraiser may perform all appraisals

TRANSFER OF PROPERTY
(Salesperson 9%/14 questions; Broker 10%/15 questions)

I.   **ALIENATION**

    A.   **Alienating property**

        1.   Means conveying property – the opposite of acquisition

        2.   Can be voluntary or involuntary

    B.   **Types of Deeds**

        Every deed conveys whatever interest is held by the grantor, unless it specifically states that it is conveying a lesser interest. The major difference between types of deeds lies in the extent of the promises given by the grantor to the grantee.

        1.   Grant Deed

            a.   Most common deed in California

            b.   Contains 2 implied warranties

                i.   Grantor has not previously conveyed the title

                ii.   Grantor has disclosed all encumbrances

            c.   May convey after-acquired title (title will be acquired by grantor at later date)

        2.   Quitclaim Deed

            a.   <u>No warranties</u>

            b.   Used as problem solver to clear a cloud on title and to terminate deed restrictions.

        3.   Warranty Deed has 5 covenants and a guarantee of title (seldom used in California because of prevalence of title insurance)

        4.   Gift Deed – given in return for "love and affection"

5.   Involuntary Deeds – must be recorded to be effective

      a.   Sheriff's Deed -- Goes to high bidder at sheriff's sale

      b.   Tax Deed – Conveys title after tax sale

      c.   Trustee's Deed – Conveys title after private foreclosure sale

C.   Essential Elements of a Valid Deed

1.   In writing

2.   Signed by grantor

3.   Competent grantor

4.   Granting Clause (Words of conveyance)

5.   Adequate description of property

6.   Must designate a grantee

NOT REQUIRED: date, signature of grantee, legal description, Habendum Clause ("to have and to hold")

D.   Essentials for a Valid Transfer

1.   Valid deed

2.   Delivered – must pass out of control of grantor during his or her lifetime; controlled by the intention of the grantor to convey property

3.   Accepted by grantee(s) – evidenced by possession of deed, encumbering title, or any act demonstrating ownership, such as taking possession

E.   Conveyance after death

1.   Probate is the judicial process to prove or confirm validity of a will, collect assets, pay debts and taxes, and distribute all of a deceased's assets

2.   Devise is the act of transferring deceased's (called the devisor or testator) interest in real estate to another (devisee) by will

3.   If intestate, laws of descent and intestate succession determine heirs/descendents

4.   <u>Court determines licensee's commission</u> if a property is sold through probate

F.   Involuntary Alienation

1.   <u>Adverse possession</u> is ownership granted by the courts due to actual, open, continuous, hostile, notorious, and exclusive possession of another's land for 5 years under claim of right or color of title. Must pay taxes for 5 years

2.   <u>Easement by prescription/prescriptive easement</u> is an easement gained through adverse possession. <u>Terminates due to non-use after 5 years</u>

3.   <u>Easement by necessity</u> is an easement created by law to prevent landlocked property. Gives grantee an easement over grantor's land, but only if there is no other access to grantee's land.

G.   Public Transfer

1.   State transfers ownership to private party by land patent or <u>patent deed</u>

2.   A conveyance of property from a private party to the state is a <u>dedication</u>

H. **Recording**

    1.   Generally not required for validity (although involuntary transfers require recording to be effective)

    2.   Gives constructive (legal) notice to protect interests (taking possession also gives constructive notice)

    3.   Can determine priority (1st in time, 1st in right)

    4.   Record in the county where property is located

II. **TITLE INSURANCE**

A. **Buyer's Goal is to Obtain Marketable (Merchantable) Title**

B. **Title Insurance**

    1.   Examiner checks abstract of title for history of conveyances and traces chain of title

    2.   <u>Certificate of title</u> lists current title status and encumbrances, and certifies that records are accurate as recorded

    3.   Preliminary report is an offer to issue a policy based on the conditions of the report

    4.   Types of policies

        a.   Standard (CLTA)

            i.   Usually protects owner

            ii.   Includes forgery and fraud, matters of record, improper delivery, lack of capacity

            iii.   Excludes items that would require a physical inspections (unrecorded mechanic's liens, encroachments, etc.)

      b.   Extended policy (ALTA)

          i.   Usually required by lenders

          ii.   Includes unrecorded liens, encroachments, rights of parties in possession, etc.

          iii.   Physical inspection is necessary

5.   <u>Zoning ordinances are NOT insurable</u>

6.   Premium paid once at the time the policy is issued

III.   ESCROW/SETTLEMENT/CLOSING

A.   Escrow/Settlement Procedures

1.   Escrow or settlement is the means by which parties to a contract carry out the terms of their agreement

2.   Parties appoint a third party to act as an escrow agent; usually a title company

3.   Seller's deed and buyer's money are deposited with escrow agent according to an escrow agreement that sets forth conditions to be met before the sale will be consummated

4.   Once in escrow, funds can be released upon written instructions of <u>both parties</u> (mutual release papers), through court action (<u>interpleader</u>), or through a <u>binding arbitration</u> decision

5.   If purchase agreement and escrow instructions disagree, <u>escrow instructions would prevail</u> because they would be the later contract

6.   During escrow, the escrow agent is a dual agent, representing both parties in the transaction. Once the transaction closes, the escrow agent is the <u>single agent of each party</u> for any remaining issues pertaining to the parties

7.   Escrow agent collects reports required for the transaction

- Termite reports are public reports and are available to <u>anyone</u> upon request

8.   A "complete escrow" is where all instructions have been completed but transaction has not yet closed

B.   Closing Statement – Debits and Credits

1.   Credit to seller is anything that increases the amount of money seller takes from the closing. Example: Sale price; pre-paid taxes

2.   Debit to seller is anything that decreases amount of money seller takes from the closing. Example: Brokerage fee, mortgage payoff

3.   Credit to buyer is anything that decreases the amount of money buyer must bring to closing. Example: Earnest money, new mortgage

4.   Debit to buyer is anything that increases the amount of money buyer must bring to the closing. Example: <u>sale price</u>, discount points (if paid by buyer)

5.   Pro-ration based on 360-day year (30 day months). Rent is paid in advance/mortgage interest is paid in arrears

6.   Insurance may be <u>short-rated</u> – when policy is cancelled prior to its expiration

Sample Question:

Green paid $77,000 for a home in a real estate transaction. The lender would lend 80% of the $75,000 value. If the buyer was charge 3% of the selling price for closing costs and he or she made a $1,200 cash downpayment, what additional amount of money would be needed in order to complete the transaction?

  a. $13,490
  b. $15,800
  c. $18,110
  d. None of the above

IV.   TAX ASPECTS

A.   Property Taxes - "At Value" - "Ad Valorem"

1.   Assessment roll establishes the tax base

2.   Properties can be re-assessed for current value and improvements. Re-assessments can be appealed to an Assessor's Appeal Board

3.   Fiscal year for property taxes begins on July 1st

  a.   First installment covering July 1st to December 31st is due November 1st

  b.   Second installment covering January 1st to June 30th is due February 1st

B.   Special Assessments

1.   Taxes charged against specific properties that benefit from a public improvement

2.   Paid along with property taxes and enforced by a lien

C. **Mello-Roos Community Facilities Act of 1982**

    1.   Created a special form of property assessment involving an improvement bond; does not appear on property tax bill

    2.   <u>Seller</u> of 1-4 unit dwelling must disclose if property is subject to a Mello-Roos lien

D. **Documentary Transfer Tax**

City or county tax rate of .55 per $500 <u>or fraction thereof</u> of purchase price

[handwritten: 500,000 / 400,000 / 100,000 X .55 / 500]

E. **Depreciation**

    1.   For tax purposes, non-owner-occupied residential properties can be depreciated over 27½ years

    2.   Non-residential (commercial, industrial) properties can be depreciated over 39 years

    3.   Only improvements are depreciated; never land

F. **Capital Gains Exemption for Principal Residence**

    1.   There is no tax on the first $250,000 of profit (single) or $500,000 of profit (married) from sale of principal residence

    2.   Must reside in residence 2 out of last 5 years

    3.   Exemption can be taken every two years (once in a lifetime limit no longer exists)

H. **Tax-Deferred Exchanges (1031)**

1. Sometimes called a "tax-free" exchange, this allows for the exchange of eligible properties while deferring paying taxes on the gain

2. Exchange must be of "like-kind" properties

3. Requires "balancing of equities." Exchange is almost never equal, and therefore payment of "boot" is required

4. Boot includes cash or its equivalent, or <u>mortgage relief</u> (taking on a loan with less principal owed)

5. Taxes are owed/recognized on the boot

6. <u>Easiest type of transaction is:</u> Like-kind exchange for similar mortgage amount and paying a little to balance the equities

I. <u>**Successor's Liability**</u>

1. Purchaser of a business may have successor's liability if sales taxes have not been fully paid by seller

2. Purchaser should get a certificate of clearance from the <u>Board of Equalization</u> showing that seller has paid all sales taxes due

J. **Tax Shelters**

Associated with <u>income taxes</u>

K. **Terms**

1. Basis – usually the sales price

2. Adjusted basis – Basis minus depreciation plus capital improvements

3. Realized gain/actual gain – Actual profit that is realized; taxed when received

4.   Recognized gain/taxable gain – Taxable now

5.   Deferred gain – Will be taxed at later date

Glossary

A

A.L.T.A. Title Policy

An extended coverage title insurance policy issued to owners and lenders. It expands the coverage normally given in a standard policy to include facts a physical survey would show and rights of parties in possession. A.L.T.A. stands for American Land Title Association.

ABC

The Department of Alcoholic Beverage Control (Div. 9 of the Business & Professions Code) issues licenses authorizing the sale of alcoholic beverages.

Abstract of Judgment

A summary of a court's decision. When recorded it creates a lien upon real and personal property of the judgment debtor.

Abatement of Nuisance

Extinction or termination of a nuisance.

Absolute Ownership

See Fee Simple Estate.

Abstract of Judgment

A condensation of the essential provisions of a court judgment.

Abstract of Title

A summary or digest of all transfers, conveyances, legal proceedings, and any other facts relied on as evidence of title, showing continuity of ownership, together with any other elements of record which may impair title.

Abstraction

A method of valuing land. The indicated value of. the improvement is deducted from the sale price.

Abutting

Touching or bordering such as land adjoining the land of another.

Accelerated Cost Recovery System

The system for figuring depreciation (cost recovery) for depreciable real property acquired and placed into service after January 1, 1981. (ACRS)

Accelerated Depreciation

A method of cost write- off in which depreciation allowances are greater in the first few years of ownership than in subsequent years. This permits an earlier recovery of capital and a faster tax write-off of an asset.

Acceleration Clause

A condition in a real estate financing instrument giving the lender the power to declare all sums owing lender immediately due and payable upon the happening of an event, such as sale of the property, or a delinquency in the repayment of the note.

Acceptance

The act of agreeing or consenting to the terms of an offer thereby establishing the "meeting of the minds" that is an essential element of a contract.

Access Right

The right of an owner to have ingress and egress to and from owner's property over adjoining property.

Accession

An addition to property through the efforts of man or by natural forces.

Accounts Receivable

An accounting term for money earned but not yet received.

Accretion

Accession by natural forces, e.g., alluvium.

Accrual for Depreciation

A provision in the income approach to appraisal in which a return of the investment is provided for out of the income in the capitalization rate.

Accrued Depreciation

The difference between the cost of replacement new as of the date of the appraisal and the present appraised value.

Accrued Items of Expense

Those incurred expenses which are not yet payable. The seller's accrued expenses are credited to the purchaser in a closing statement.

Accusation

A written statement delivered to the licensee by the Department of Real Estate prior to a disciplinary action hearing regarding the possible revocation or suspension of their license setting forth the acts or omissions for which they are being charged.

Acknowledgment

A formal declaration made before an authorized person, e.g., a notary public, by a person who has executed an instrument stating that the execution was his or her free act. In this state an acknowledgment is the statement by an officer such as a notary that the signatory to the instrument is the person represented to be.

Acoustical Tile

Blocks of fiber, mineral or metal, with small holes or rough-textured surface to absorb sound, used as covering for interior walls and ceilings.

Acquisition

The act or process by which a person procures property.

Acre

A measure of land equaling 160 square rods, or 4,840 square yards, or 43,560 square feet, or a tract about 208.71 feet square.

Action of the Sun

A consideration in the selection of a retail store location. The shadiest sides of the street – the south and west sides – are considered the most desirable.

Actual Authority

Authority expressly given by the principal or given by the law and not denied by the principal.

Actual Fraud

An act intended to deceive another, e.g., making a false statement, making a promise without intending to perform it, suppressing the truth.

Actual Notice

Information of a fact actually, expressly or directly given to a person.

Adjustable Rate Mortgage (ARM)

A mortgage loan which bears interest at a rate subject to change during the term of the loan, predetermined or otherwise.

Adjusted Cost Basis

The value of a property as shown on the books of a taxpayer. It is calculated from the original cost, plus any improvements less allowable depreciation.

Adjustments

In appraising, a means by which characteristics of a residential property are regulated by dollar amount or percentage to conform to similar characteristics of another residential property.

Administer

The process of arranging, processing and funding a loan as opposed to servicing the loan after it is made. Not always done by the same agency.

Administrative Procedure Act

The state law that established the procedure that the Real Estate Commissioner must follow in order to discipline a licensee.

Administrator

A person appointed by the probate court to administer the estate of a deceased person who died intestate. (Administratrix, the feminine form.)

Ad Valorem

A Latin phrase meaning "according to value." Usually used in connection with real estate taxation.

Advance

Transfer of funds from a lender to a borrower in advance on a loan.

Advance Commitment

The institutional investor's prior agreement to provide long-term financing upon completion of construction; also known as a "take- out" loan commitment.

Advance Fees

A fee paid in advance of any services rendered. Sometimes unlawfully charged in connection with that illegal practice of obtaining a fee in advance for the advertising of property or businesses for sale, with no intent to obtain a buyer, by persons representing themselves as real estate licensees, or representatives of licensed real estate firms.

Adverse Possession

A method of acquiring title to real property through possession of the property for a statutory period under certain conditions by a person other than the owner of record.

Affiant

One who makes an affidavit or gives evidence.

Affidavit

A statement or declaration reduced to writing sworn to or affirmed before some officer who has authority to administer an oath or affirmation.

Affidavit of Title

A statement, in writing, made under oath by seller or grantor, acknowledged before a Notary Public in which the affiant identifies himself or herself and affiant's marital status certifying that since the examination of title on the contract date there are no judgments, bankruptcies or divorces, no unrecorded deeds, contracts, unpaid repairs or improvements or defects of title known to affiant and that affiant is in possession of the property.

Affirm

To make a solemn declaration by one whose religious beliefs forbid the taking of oaths. To confirm, to aver, to ratify, to verify.

Affirmation

A solemn declaration by a person whose religious beliefs forbid the taking of an oath.

After Acquired Title

Defined in the Civil Code in Section 1106 as: "When a person purports by proper instrument to grant real property in fee simple and subsequently acquires any title or claim of title thereto, the same passes by operation of law to the grantee or his successors."

Agency

The relationship between principal and the principal's agent which arises out of a contract, either expressed or implied, written or oral, wherein the agent is employed by the principal to do certain acts dealing with a third party.

Agent

One who acts for and with authority from another called the principal.

Agreement

An exchange of promises, a mutual understanding or arrangement; a contract.

Agreement of Sale

A written agreement or contract between seller and purchaser in which they reach a "meeting of minds" on the terms and conditions of the sale. The parties concur; are in harmonious opinion.

Air Rights

The rights in real property to the reasonable use of the air space above the surface of the land.

Alcoholic Beverage Control Act

A California law regulating the sale of alcoholic beverages which is administered by the State Department of Alcoholic Beverage Control. Both the Act and the Department are abbreviated as ABC.

Alienation

The transferring of property to another; the transfer of property and possession of lands, or other things, from one person to another.

Alienation Clause

A clause in a contract giving the lender certain rights in the event of a sale or other transfer of mortgaged property.

All Inclusive Trust Deed

A financing device whereby a lender assumes payments on existing trust deeds of a borrower and takes a junior trust deed for the total existing debts plus the additional amount borrowed. This is also called A.I.T.D., wrap-around or wrap.

Allodial Tenure

A real property ownership system where ownership may be complete except for those rights held by government. Allodial is in contrast to feudal tenure.

Alluvium

The gradual increase of the earth on a shore of an ocean or bank of a stream resulting from the action of the water.

ALTA Owner's Policy

An owner's extended coverage policy that provides buyers and owners the same protection the ALTA policy gives to lenders.

ALTA Title Policy

(American Land Title Association) A type of title insurance policy issued by title insurance companies which expands the risks normally insured against under the standard type policy to include unrecorded mechanic's liens; unrecorded physical easements; facts a physical survey would show; water and mineral rights; and rights of parties in possession, such as tenants and buyers under unrecorded instruments.

Alternative Minimum Tax

An aspect of the federal income tax program which is a flat tax applied on an "alternative minimum taxable income" basis to ensure that everyone with income above a certain level pays some income tax.

Ambulatory

Movable. When applied to wills, it means revocable.

Amenities

Satisfaction of enjoyable living to be derived from a home; conditions of agreeable living or a beneficial influence from the location of improvements, not measured in monetary considerations but rather as tangible and intangible benefits attributable to the property, often causing greater pride in ownership.

Amenity Value

The value of the pleasures a property offers such as a good neighborhood, schools, parks, a view or other tangible or intangible assets.

Amortization

The liquidation of a financial obligation on an installment basis; also, recovery over a period of cost or value.

Amortization Table

A table showing the payments required to amortize loans at various interest rates over various periods of time.

Amortized Loan

A loan to be repaid, interest and principal, by a series of regular payments that are equal or nearly equal, without any special balloon payment prior to maturity. Also called a Level Payments Loan.

Anchor Tenant

The key tenant in a commercial development such as a mall. The quality of this tenant often determines the size of a loan that can be secured.

Annexation

An addition to property by the act of attaching a smaller thing to the larger property usually by attaching personal property to real property.

Annual Percentage Rate

The relative cost of credit as determined in accordance with Regulation Z of the Board of Governors of the Federal Reserve System for implementing the Federal Truth in Lending Act.

Annuity

A sum of money received at fixed intervals, such as a series of assured equal or nearly equal payments to be made over a period of time, or it may be a lump sum payment to be made in the future. The installment payments due to the landlord under a lease is an annuity. So are the installment payments due to a lender.

Anticipation, Principle of

Affirms that value is created by anticipated benefits to be derived in the future.

Appellant

A party appealing a court decision or ruling.

Appraisal

An estimate of the value of property resulting from an analysis of facts about the property. An opinion of value.

Appraiser

One qualified by education, training and experience who is hired to estimate the value of real and personal property based on experience, judgment, facts, and use of formal appraisal processes.

Appreciation

Increase in value due to any cause.

Appropriation of Water

The taking, impounding or diversion of water flowing on the public domain from its natural course and the application of the water to some beneficial use personal and exclusive to the appropriator.

Appurtenance:

That which belongs to something, but not immemorially; all those rights, privileges, and improvements which belong to and pass with the transfer of the property, but which are not necessarily a part of the actual property. Appurtenances to real property pass with the real property to which they are appurtenant, unless a contrary intention is manifested. Typical appurtenances are rights-of-way, easements, water rights, and any property improvements.

Appurtenant

Belonging to; adjunct; appended or annexed to. For example, the garage is appurtenant to the house, and the common interest in the common elements of a condominium is appurtenant to each apartment. Appurtenant items pass with the land when the property is transferred.

APR

See Annual Percentage Rate.

Architectural Style

Generally the appearance and character of a building's design and construction.

Arranger of Credit

Defined by California Civil Code as "a party to the transaction" who is a real estate licensee or attorney or a non-attorney who arranges credit extended by a seller. This person is responsible for the disclosure statements required when credit is extended by a seller of residential property. Under California law it is a person who arranges credit in a seller-carry-back transaction as an agent or a principal who has a R.E. license or is an attorney. That arranger of credit must supply a disclosure statement in residential sales which have been improved (i.e. with buildings).

Article 5

The part of the California Real Estate Law that regulates transactions in notes and land contracts.

Article 7

A part of the California Real Estate Law known as the Broker Loan Law which sets maximum limits on commissions, costs and expenses for certain broker-negotiated loans.

Articles of Incorporation

An instrument setting forth the basic rules and purposes under which a private corporation is formed.

Assemblage

Combining two or more parcels into one large tract. The end result is usually in some greater value than the sum of the individual parcels. The increase in value is called plottage or plottage increment.

Assessed Valuation

A valuation placed upon a piece of property by a public authority as a basis for levying taxes on the property.

Assessment

The valuation of property for the purpose of levying a tax or the amount of the tax levied. Also, payments made to a common interest subdivision homeowners- association for maintenance and reserves.

Assessor

The official who has the responsibility of determining assessed values.

Assets

Anything of value owned.

Assign

The transfer of the right, title and interest in the property of one party, the assignor to another party, the assignee.

Assignment

A transfer to another of any property in possession or in action, or of any estate or right therein. A transfer by a person of that person's rights under a contract.

Assignment of Rents

A provision in a deed of trust (or mortgage) under which the beneficiary may, upon default by the trustor, take possession of the property, collect income from the property and apply it to the loan balance and the costs incurred by the beneficiary.

Assignor

One who assigns or transfers property.

Assigns, Assignees

Those to whom property or interests therein shall have been transferred.

Associate Licensee

A broker or salesperson employed by a real estate broker.

Assumed Name

A name used other than a person's legal name.

Assumption

Taking over the primary liability for the payment of an existing trust deed or mortgage.

Assumption Agreement

An undertaking or adoption of a debt or obligation primarily resting upon another person.

Assumption Fee

A lender's charge for changing over and processing new records for a new owner who is assuming an existing loan.

Assumption of Mortgage

The taking of a title to property by a grantee wherein grantee assumes liability for payment of an existing note secured by a mortgage or deed of trust against the property, becoming a coguarantor for the payment of a mortgage or deed of trust note.

Attachment

The process by which real or personal property of a party to a lawsuit is seized and retained in the custody of the court for the purpose of acquiring jurisdiction over the property, to compel an appearance before the court, or to furnish security for a debt or costs arising out of the litigation.

Attest

To affirm to be true or genuine; an official act establishing authenticity.

Attorney In Fact

One who is authorized by another to perform certain acts for another under a power of attorney; power of attorney may be limited to a specific act or acts or be general.

Authorization to Sell

A shorter name for the Exclusive Authorization and Right to Sell– commonly called a listing.

Avulsion

A sudden and perceptible loss of land by the action of water as by a sudden change in the course of a river.

B

Backfill

The replacement of excavated earth into a hole or against a structure.

Bailiff

A court attendant, usually a sheriff's officer or deputy.

Bailment

A delivery of personal property in trust for a certain purpose with a contract, express or implied, that the property will be returned or accounted for when the purpose is accomplished.

Balance

An appraisal principle that holds that value is created and maintained when contrasting, opposing, or interacting elements are in a state of equilibrium. Value is sustained when the four "agents in the production of income" are in proper balance.

Balance Sheet

A statement of the financial condition of a business at a certain time showing assets, liabilities, and capital.

Balloon Payment

An installment payment on a promissory note usually the final. one for discharging the debt which is significantly larger than the other installment payments provided under the terms of the promissory note.

Band of Investment

A method of developing a capitalization rate by combining the weighted average rates attributable to the different components of invested capital.

Banker's Rule

The convention that for proration and some other calculations a month consists of 30 days and a year of 360 days.

Bargain and Sale Deed

Any deed that recites a consideration and purports to convey the real estate; a bargain and sale deed with a covenant against the grantor's act is one in which the grantor warrants that grantor has done nothing to harm or cloud the title.

Barred

Obstructed by a barrier that will prevent legal recovery. For example, an action is barred by the Statute of Limitations if the time has lapsed during which one may assert their legal right.

Base and Meridian

Imaginary lines used by surveyors to find and describe the location of private or public lands. In government surveys, a base line runs due east and west, meridians run due north and south, and are used to establish township boundaries

Base Line

A survey line running east and west used in establishing township boundaries.

Basis

(1) Cost Basis-The dollar amount assigned to property at the time of acquisition under provisions of the Internal Revenue Code for the purpose of determining gain, loss and depreciation in calculating the income tax to be paid upon the sale or exchange of the property. (2) Adjusted Cost Basis-The cost basis after the application of certain additions for improvements, etc., and deductions for depreciation, etc.

Bearing Wall

A wall or partition which supports a part of a building, usually a roof or floor above.

Bench Mark

A monument used to establish the elevation of the point, usually relative to Mean Sea Level, but often to some local datum.

Beneficiary

(1) One entitled to the benefit of a trust; (2) One who receives profit from an estate, the title of which is vested in a trustee; (3) The lender on the security of a note and deed of trust.

Beneficiary Statement

The statement of a lender giving the remaining principal balance and other information concerning a loan. It is usually obtained when a borrower wishes to sell, pay off a loan or refinance.

Bequeath

To give or hand down personal property by will; to leave by will. Real property is "devised," not "bequeathed."

Bequest

Personal property given by the terms of a will.

Betterment

An improvement upon property which increases the property value and is considered as a capital asset as distinguished from repairs or replacements where the original character or cost is unchanged.

Bilateral

Two-sided. A bilateral contract is a contract in which a promise is given in exchange for a promise. It obligates both sides.

Blind Advertising

Failure by a licensee to indicate license status in any advertising of services for which a real estate license is required.

Bill of Sale

A written instrument given to pass title of personal property from vendor to the vendee.

Binder

An agreement to consider a down payment for the purchase of real estate as evidence of good faith on the part of the purchaser. Also, a notation of coverage on an insurance policy, issued by an agent, and given to the insured prior to issuing of the policy.

Blanket Mortgage

A single mortgage which covers more than one piece of real property.

Blighted Area

A district affected by detrimental influences of such extent or quantity that real property values have seriously declined as a result of adverse land use and/or destructive economic forces; characterized by rapidly depreciating buildings, retrogression and no recognizable prospects for improvement. However, renewal programs and changes in use may lead to resurgence of such areas.

Blockbusting

The practice on the part of unscrupulous speculators or real estate agents of inducing panic selling of homes at prices below market value, especially by exploiting the prejudices of property owners in neighborhoods in which the racial make-up is changing or appears to be on the verge of changing.

Board of Equalization

The state agency that determines assessed value of public utility properties, supervises county assessors and tax collectors in order to create uniformity in tax assessment and collects state sales taxes.

Bona Fide

In good faith; without fraud or deceit; authentic.

Bond

Written evidence of an obligation given by a corporation or government entity. A surety instrument.

Book Value

The current value for accounting purposes of an asset expressed as original cost plus capital additions minus accumulated depreciation.

Boot

Something not of like kind received in a tax-deferred exchange such as cash or equivalent, or net mortgage relief.

Bracketing

The selecting of a value that falls within the highs and lows of recent selling prices of comparable properties. It is used in the market data approach.

Breach

The breaking of a law, or failure of duty, either by omission or commission.

Broker

A person employed for a fee by another to carry on any of the activities listed in the license law definition of a broker.

Broker's Loan Statement

A statement given to the borrower at the time of a loan transaction negotiated by a licensee, indicating the costs, expenses and deductions of the loan. Also called a mortgage loan disclosure statement.

Broker-Salesperson Relationship Agreement

A written agreement required by the regulations of the Real Estate Commissioner setting forth the material aspects of the relationship between a real estate broker and each salesperson and broker performing licensed activities in the name of the supervising broker.

B.T.U. British Thermal Unit

The quantity of heat required to raise the temperature of one pound of water one degree Fahrenheit.

Building Code

A systematic regulation of construction of buildings within a municipality established by ordinance or law.

Building Line

A line set by law a certain distance from a street line in front of which an owner cannot build on owner's lot. A setback line.

Building, Market Value of

The sum of money which the presence of that structure adds to or subtracts from the value of the land it occupies. Land valued on the basis of highest and best use.

Building Residual Technique

A method in appraising of determining the contribution of an improvement to the present value of the entire property.

Building Restrictions

Zoning, regulatory requirements or provisions in a deed limiting the type, size and use of a building.

Bulk Sales Law

Bulk Sales Law is Division 6 of the Uniform Commercial Code that regulates the sale of inventory of a business for the protection of the seller's creditors and the buyer.

Bundle of Rights

All of the legal rights incident to ownership of property including rights of use, possession, encumbering and disposition.

Bureau of Land Management

A federal bureau within the Department of the Interior which manages and controls certain lands owned by the United States.

Business and Professions Code

The body of laws containing the California Real Estate Law and other state licensing laws.

Business Opportunity

The assets for an existing business enterprise including its goodwill. As used in the Real Estate Law, the term includes "the sale or lease of the business and goodwill of an existing business enterprise or opportunity."

Buydown

See Subsidy Buydown.

C

Cal-vet Program

A program administered by the State Department of Veterans Affairs for the direct financing of farm and home purchases by eligible California veterans of the armed forces.

CC&Rs

Covenants, conditions and restrictions. The basic rules establishing the rights and obligations of owners (and their successors in interest) of real property within a subdivision or other tract of land in relation to other owners within the same subdivision or tract and in relation to an association of owners organized for the purpose of operating and maintaining property commonly owned by the individual owners.

CCIM

Certified Commercial Investment Member.

CPM°

Certified Property Manager, a designation of the Institute of Real Estate Management.

California Department of Veterans Affairs

The state agency that, among other things, makes Cal-Vet loans to qualified veterans.

Called Loan

A loan that is due and payable at the demand of the lender usually as a result of an acceleration or alienation clause becoming effective.

Buyer's Market

The condition which exists when a buyer is in a more commanding position as to price and terms because real property offered for sale is in plentiful supply in relation to demand.

By-laws

Rules for the conduct of the internal affairs of corporations and other organizations.

Capacity

The legal ability of a person or entity to enter into a contract that is legally binding and to perform certain other civil acts such as making a will.

Capital Assets

Assets of a permanent nature used in the production of an income, such as land, buildings, machinery and equipment, etc. Under income tax law, it is usually distinguishable from "inventory" which comprises assets held for sale to customers in ordinary course of the taxpayer's trade or business.

Capital Expenditures

The cost of a capital improvement such as investments in land, buildings, machinery, and equipment.

Capital Gain

At resale of a capital item, the amount by which the net sale proceeds exceed the adjusted cost basis (book value). Used for income tax computations. Gains are called short or long term based upon length of holding period after acquisition. Usually taxed at lower rates than ordinary income.

Capitalization

In appraising, determining value of property by considering net income and percentage of reasonable return on the investment. The value of an income property is determined by dividing annual net income by the Capitalization Rate.

Capitalization Rate

The rate of interest which is considered a reasonable return on the investment, and used in the process of determining value based upon net income. It may also be described as the yield rate that is necessary to attract the money of the average investor to a particular kind of investment. In the case of land improvements which depreciate, to this yield rate is added a factor to take into consideration the annual amortization factor necessary to recapture the initial investment in improvements. This amortization factor can be determined in various ways (1). straight-line depreciation method, (2) Inwood Tables and (3) Hoskold Tables. (To explore this subject in greater depth, the student should refer to current real estate appraisal texts.)

Cap Rate

See Life of Loan Cap.

Carryback Financing

Financing in which the seller takes back a note for part of the purchase price secured by a junior trust deed, a wraparound mortgage or a contract for deed.

Casement Windows

Frames of wood or metal which swing outward.

Cash Disbursements Journal

A record of all cash payments.

Cash Flow

The net income generated by a property before depreciation and other noncash expenses.

Cash Receipts Journal

A record of all funds received.

Caveat Emptor

Let the buyer beware. The buyer must examine the goods or property and buy at his or her own risk, absent misrepresentation.

Certificate of Clearance

A certificate obtained from the State Board of Equalization showing that no sales tax is due from the seller of a business. It protects the buyer from successor's liability. It is also called a clearance receipt.

Certificate of Eligibility

Issued by Department of Veterans Affairs evidence of individual's eligibility to obtain VA loan.

Certificate of Reasonable Value (CRV)

The Federal VA appraisal commitment of property value.

Certificate of Sale

A certificate issued to the purchaser at a judicial mortgage foreclosure sale granting the purchaser title which under certain circumstances may be subsequently redeemed by the borrower, but not necessarily possession to the property purchased.

Certificate of Taxes Due

A written statement or guaranty of the condition of the taxes on a certain property made by the County Treasurer of the county wherein the property is located. Any loss resulting to any person from an error in a tax certificate shall be paid by the county which such treasurer represents.

Certificate of Title

A written opinion by an attorney that ownership of the particular parcel of land is as stated in the certificate.

Certiorari

A review by a an appellate court of a case or proceeding conducted by an inferior court, officer, board or tribunal to certify the record of such proceeding. A means of obtaining further information and a judicial review in a pending case.

Chain

A unit of measurement used by surveyors. A chain consists of 100 links equal to 66 feet.

Chain of Title

A history of conveyances and encumbrances affecting the title from the time the original patent was granted, or as far back as records are available, used to determine how title came to be vested in current owner.

Change, Principle of

Holds that it is the future, not the past, which is of prime importance in estimating value. Change is largely result of cause and effect.

Characteristics

Distinguishing features of a (residential) property.

Character of Soil

The nature of land. Soil may be sandy, adobe, rocky, fertile, etc.

Chattel Mortgage

A claim on personal property (instead of real property) used to secure or guarantee a promissory note. (See definition of Security Agreement and Security Interest.)

Chattel Real

An estate related to real estate, such as a lease on real property.

Chattels

Goods or every species of property movable or immovable which are not real property. Personal property.

Chose

A French word meaning *thing* used as a legal term for an article of personal property. "Chose in possession" is tangible personal property and "chose in action" is intangible personal property.

Chose In Action

A personal right to something not presently in the owner's possession, but recoverable by a legal action for possession.

Chronological Age

The age of a property determined by the number of years since the structure was built.

Circuit Breaker

(1) An electrical device which automatically interrupts an electric circuit when an overload occurs; may be used instead of a fuse to protect each circuit and can be reset. (2) In property taxation, a method for granting property tax relief to the elderly and disadvantaged qualified taxpayers by rebate, tax credits or cash payments. Usually limited to homeowners and renters.

Claim of Right

An aspect of adverse possession or easement by prescription whereby a person occupies property even though having no legalright to title, but nevertheless claiming such a right under a claim of right—when the adverse user or possessor treats the land as his or her own, or under a color of title—when they have some reason to believe that they have title.

Client

The person represented by an agent who could be a broker or an attorney.

Closing

(1) Process by which all the parties to a real estate transaction conclude the details of a sale or mortgage. The process includes the signing and transfer of documents and distribution of funds. (2) Condition in description of real property by courses and distances at the boundary lines where the lines meet to include all the tract of land.

Closing Costs

The miscellaneous expenses buyers and sellers normally incur in the transfer of ownership of real property over and above the cost of the property.

Closing Statement

An accounting of funds made to the buyer and seller separately. Required by law to be made at the completion of every real estate transaction.

Cloud on Title

A claim, encumbrance or condition which impairs the title to real property until disproved or eliminated as for example through a quitclaim deed or a quiet title legal action.

Code of Ethics

A set of rules and principles expressing a standard of accepted conduct for a professional group and governing the relationship of members to each other and to the organization.

Codicil

A supplement, addition or change to a will that usually does not revoke the entire will.

Collateral

Marketable real or personal property which a borrower pledges as security for a loan. In mortgage transactions, specific land is the collateral. (See definition of Security Interest.)

Collateral Security

A separate obligation attached to contract to guarantee its performance; the transfer of property or of other contracts, or valuables, to insure the performance of a principal agreement.

Collusion

An agreement between two or more persons to defraud another of rights by the forms of law, or to obtain an object forbidden by law.

Color of Title

That which appears to be good title but which is not title in fact.

Commercial Acre

A term applied to the remainder of an acre of newly subdivided land after the area devoted to streets, sidewalks and curbs, etc., has been deducted from the acre.

Commercial Loan

A personal loan from a commercial bank, usually unsecured and short term, for other than mortgage purposes.

Commercial Paper

Negotiable instruments such as promissory notes, letters of credit and bills of lading. Instruments developed under the law of merchant.

Commingling

Unauthorized mixing of personal funds with funds of a client or customer, i.e. putting the client's funds into the broker's personal account.

Commission

An agent's compensation for performing the duties of the agency; in real estate practice, a percentage of the selling price of property, percentage of rentals, etc. A fee for services.

Commissioner's Regulations

Regulations adopted by the Real Estate Commissioner to implement the California Real Estate Law. They have the force and effect of the law itself, and are contained in the Commissioner's Code of Regulations.

Commitment

A pledge or a promise or firm agreement to do something in the future, such as a loan company giving a written commitment with specific terms of mortgage loan it will make.

Common Area

An entire common interest subdivision except the separate interests therein.

Common Interest Subdivision

Subdivided lands which include a separate interest in real property combined with an interest in common with other owners. The interest in common may be through membership in an association. Examples are condominiums and stock cooperatives.

Common Law

The body of law that grew from customs and practices developed and used in England "since the memory of man runneth not to the contrary."

Common Stock

That class of corporate stock to which there is ordinarily attached no preference with respect to the receipt of dividends or the distribution of assets on corporate dissolution.

Community Apartment Project

Multiple ownership of an unincorporated apartment building in which each owner is a tenant in common and has the right to occupy one of the apartments.

Community Property

Property acquired by husband and/or wife during a marriage when not acquired as the separate property of either spouse. Each spouse has equal rights of management, alienation and testamentary disposition of community property.

Compaction

Whenever extra soil is added to a lot to fill in low places or to raise the level of the lot, the added soil is often too loose and soft to sustain the weight of the buildings. Therefore, it is necessary to compact the added soil so that it will carry the weight of buildings without the danger of their tilting, settling or cracking.

Comparable Sales

Sales which have similar characteristics as the subject property and are used for analysis in the appraisal process. Commonly called "comparables", they are recent selling prices of properties similarly situated in a similar market.

Comparative Analysis

A method of appraisal in which selling prices of similar properties are used as the basis for arriving at the value estimate. It is also known as the market data approach.

Comparison Approach

A real estate comparison method which compares a given property with similar or comparable surrounding properties; also called market comparison.

Compensating Balance

A commercial bank's requirement that the borrower keep a specified amount of funds on deposit in the institution as a condition of the loan or line of credit.

Compensation

Money or equivalent of money received for services rendered.

Competent

Legally qualified.

Competition, Principle of

Holds that profits tend to breed competition and excess profits tend to breed ruinous completion.

Completion Bond

A bond guaranteeing the proposed construction of an improvement for which a lender advances money to the owner will be completed according to specifications and free and clear of all mechanics liens.

Compound Interest

Interest paid on original principal and also on the accrued and unpaid interest which has Accumulated As The Debt Matures.

Conclusion

The final estimate of value, realized from facts, data, experience and judgment, set out in an appraisal. Appraiser's certified conclusion.

Condemnation

The act of taking private property for public use by a political subdivision upon payment to owner of just compensation. Declaration that a structure is unfit for use.

Condition

In contracts, a future and uncertain event which must happen to create an obligation or which extinguishes an existent obligation. In conveyances of real property conditions in the conveyance may cause an interest to be vested or defeated.

Condition Precedent

A qualification of a contract or transfer of property, providing that unless and until a given event occurs, the full effect of a contract or transfer will not take place.

Condition Subsequent

A condition attached to an already-vested estate or to a contract whereby the estate is defeated or the contract extinguished through the failure or non-performance of the condition.

Conditional Commitment

A commitment of a definite loan amount for some future unknown purchaser of satisfactory credit standing.

Conditional Estate

Usually called, in California, Fee Simple Defeasible. An estate that is granted subject to a condition subsequent. The estate is terminable on happening of the condition.

Conditional Sale Contract

A contract for the sale of property staffing that delivery is to be made to the buyer, title to remain vested in the seller until the conditions of the contract have been fulfilled. (See definition of Security Interest.)

Condominium

An estate in real property wherein there is an undivided interest in common in a portion of real property coupled with a separate interest in space called a unit, the boundaries of which are described on a recorded final map, parcel map or condominium plan. The areas within the boundaries may be filled with air, earth, or water or any combination and need not be attached to land except by easements for access and support.

Condominium Declaration

The document which establishes a condominium and describes the property rights of the unit owners.

Confession of Judgment

An entry of judgment upon the debtor's voluntary admission or confession.

Confirmation of Sale

A court approval of the sale of property by an executor, administrator, guardian or conservator.

Confiscation

The seizing of property without compensation.

Conformity, Principle of

Holds that the maximum of value is realized when a reasonable degree of homogeneity of improvements is present. Use conformity is desirable, creating and maintaining higher values.

Consent

Agreement to do or not to do something. Mutual consent of all parties is one of the four essential elements of any valid contract.

Conservation

The process of utilizing resources in such a manner which minimizes their depletion.

Conservator

A person appointed by the court to administer the person and property of another to ensure that the property will be properly managed.

Consideration

Anything given or promised by a party to induce another to enter into a contract, e.g., personal services or even love and affection. It may be a benefit conferred upon one party or a detriment suffered by the other.

Conspicuousness

A factor of publicity value, of great importance to a business dependent upon advertising.

Constant

The percentage which, when applied directly to the face value of a debt, develops the annual amount of money necessary to pay a specified net rate of interest on the reducing balance and to liquidate the debt in a specified time period. For example, a 6% loan with a 20 year amortization has a constant of approximately 8 1/2%. Thus, a $10,000 loan amortized over 20 years requires an annual payment of approximately $850.00.

Construction Loan

A loan made to finance the actual construction or improvement on land. Funds are usually dispersed in increments as the construction progresses.

Constructive Eviction

Breach of a covenant of warranty or quiet enjoyment, e.g., the inability of a lessee to obtain possession because of a paramount defect in title or a condition making occupancy hazardous.

Constructive Fraud

A breach of duty, as by a person in a fiduciary capacity, without an actual fraudulent intent, which gains an advantage to the person at fault by misleading another to the other's prejudice. Any act of omission declared by law to be fraudulent, without respect to actual fraud.

Constructive Notice

Notice of the condition of title to real property given by the official records of a government entity which does not require actual knowledge of the information.

Constructive Severance

A way of separating fixtures or appurtenances from land. Sale or mortgaging of crops before harvesting (before severance) is a constructive severance, converting the crops into personal property. Parties may create a constructive severance of fixtures by contract.

Contiguous

In close proximity.

Contingency

A future event or condition upon which a valid contract is dependent.

Continuation Statement

The statement filed with the California Secretary of State to extend the time limit on a previously filed *financing statement.*

Contour

The surface configuration of land. Shown on maps as a line through points of equal elevation.

Contract

An agreement to do or not to do a certain thing. It must have four essential elements parties capable of contracting, consent of the parties, a lawful object, and consideration. A contract for sale of real property must also be in writing and signed by the party or parties to be charged with performance.

Contract Rent

The rent set forth in a lease.

Contribution, Principle of

A component part of a property is valued in proportion to its contribution to the value of the whole. Holds that maximum values are achieved when the improvements on a site produce the highest (net) return, commensurate with the investment.

Controller's Deed

A deed issued by the state, usually when property is sold due to tax delinquency.

Conventional Mortgage

A mortgage securing a loan made by investors without governmental underwriting, i.e., which is not FHA insured or VA guaranteed. The type customarily made by a bank or savings and loan association.

Conversion

(1) Change from one legal form or use to another, as converting an apartment building to condominium use. (2) The unlawful appropriation of another's property, as in the conversion of trust funds.

Convey

To transfer title to property from one person to another.

Conveyance

An instrument in writing used to transfer (convey) title to property from one person to another, such as a deed or a trust deed.

Cooperative (apartment)

An apartment building, owned by a corporation and in which tenancy in an apartment unit is obtained by purchase of shares of the stock of the corporation and where the owner of such shares is entitled to occupy a specific apartment in the building. In California, this type of ownership is called a "stock cooperative."

Corner Influence Table

A statistical table that may be used to estimate the added value of a corner lot.

Corporate Securities Dealer

A person authorized to engage in the sale of common stock, preferred stock or bonds of a corporation.

Corporation

An entity established and treated by law as an individual or unit with rights and liabilities, or both, distinct and apart from those of the persons composing it. A corporation is a creature of law having certain powers and duties of a natural person. Being created by law it may continue for any length of time the law prescribes.

Corporeal Rights

Possessory rights in real property.

Correction Lines

A system for compensating inaccuracies in the Government Rectangular Survey System due to the curvature of the earth. Every fourth township line, 24 mile intervals, is used as a correction line on which the intervals between the north and south range lines are remeasured and corrected to a full 6 miles.

Correlation

A step in the appraisal process involving the interpretation of data derived from the three approaches to value (cost, market and income) leading to a single determination of value. Also frequently referred to as "reconciliation."

Co-signer

A second party who signs a promissory note together with the primary borrower.

Cost

The amount expended (in labor, material and/or money) to acquire or produce a commodity or property.

Cost Approach

One of three methods in the appraisal process. An analysis in which a value estimate of a property is derived by estimating the replacement cost of the improvements, deducting therefrom the estimated accrued depreciation, then adding the market value of the land.

Cost Basis

Original acquisition price plus acquisition expense or the original book value. Used for income tax purposes.

Cotenancy

Ownership of an interest in a particular parcel of land by more than one person; e.g. tenancy in common, joint tenancy.

Covenant

An agreement or promise to do or not to do a particular act such as a promise to build a house of a particular architectural style or to use or not use property in a certain way.

Co-venture Loan

Another name for Equity Participation Loan. The lender gets a share of ownership or income from the property.

Crawl Hole

Exterior or interior opening permitting access underneath building, as required by building codes.

CRE

Counselor of Real Estate, Member of American Society of Real Estate Counselors.

Credit

A bookkeeping entry on the right side of an account, recording the reduction or elimination of an asset or an expense, or the creation of or addition to a liability or item of equity or revenue.

Cubic Foot

A volume equivalent to a cube whose length, width and height are each one foot. 1,728 cubic inches.

Cubic Yard

A volume equivalent to a cube whose length, width and height are each one yard. 27 cubic feet.

Curable Depreciation

Items of physical deterioration and functional obsolescence which are customarily repaired or replaced by a prudent property owner.

Current Index

With regard to an adjustable rate mortgage, the current value of a recognized index as calculated and published nationally or regionally. The current index value changes periodically and is used in calculating the new note rate as of each rate adjustment date.

Curtail Schedule

A listing of the amounts by which the principal sum of an obligation is to be reduced by partial payments and of the dates when each payment Will Become Payable.

Customer

A prospective third party often a buyer, but not a client.

D

Damages

The indemnity recoverable by a person who has sustained an injury, either in his or her person, property, or relative rights, through the act or default of another. Loss sustained or harm done to a person or property.

Data Plant

An appraiser's file of information on real estate.

DBA

An abbreviation for "doing business as," a fictitious business name.

Debenture

Bonds issued without security, an obligation not secured by a specific lien on property.

Debit

A bookkeeping entry on the left side of an account, recording the creation of or addition to an asset or an expense, or the reduction or elimination of a liability or item of equity or revenue.

Debt

That which is due from one person or another; obligation, liability.

Debtor

A person who is in debt; the one owing money to another.

Deciduous

Falling off, as with trees that annually shed their leaves.

Declaration of Abandonment

The document recorded to terminate a homestead.

Declaration of Homestead

The document recorded to create a homestead.

Declining Balance Depreciation

A method of accelerated depreciation allowed by the IRS in certain circumstances. Double Declining Balance Depreciation is its most common form and is computed by using double the rate used for straight line depreciation.

Decree

A court order.

Decree of Foreclosure

Decree by a court ordering the sale of mortgaged property and the payment of the debt owing to the lender out of the proceeds.

Dedication

The giving of land by its owner to a public use and the acceptance for such use by authorized officials on behalf of the public.

Deed

Written instrument which when properly executed and delivered conveys title to real property from one person (grantor) to another (grantee).

Deed in Lieu of Foreclosure

A deed to real property accepted by a lender from a defaulting borrower to avoid the necessity of foreclosure proceedings by the lender.

Deed of Trust

(See Trust Deed.)

Deed Restrictions

Limitations in the deed to a property that dictate certain uses that may or may not be made of the property.

Default

Failure to fulfill a duty or promise or to discharge an obligation; omission or failure to perform any act.

Default Judgment

A court order resulting from the failure of a defendant to answer a complaint in a lawsuit.

Defeasance Clause

The clause in a mortgage that gives the mortgagor the right to redeem mortgagor's property upon the payment of mortgagor's obligations to the mortgagee.

Defeasible Fee

Sometimes called a base fee or qualified fee; a fee simple absolute interest in land that is capable of being defeated or terminated upon the happening of a specified event.

Defendant

A person against whom legal action is initiated for the purpose of obtaining criminal sanctions (criminal defendant) or damages or other appropriate judicial relief (civil defendant).

Deferred Gain

Gain that does not have to be *recognized* in a given tax year so that the tax on that gain can be deferred to a subsequent year.

Deferred Maintenance

Existing but unfulfilled requirements for repairs and rehabilitation. Postponed or delayed maintenance causing decline in a building's physical condition.

Deferred Payment Options

The privilege of deferring income payments to take advantage of statutes affording tax benefits.

Deficiency Judgment

A judgment given by a court when the value of security pledged for a loan is insufficient to pay off the debt of the defaulting borrower.

Deficit Financing

The purchase of income property where the net income is not sufficient to cover the payments on the property.

Delegation of Powers

The conferring by an agent upon another of all or certain of the powers that have been conferred upon the agent by the principal.

Demand

One of the four essential elements of value – the willingness of consumers to buy goods or services at a given price.

Demise

The transfer to another of an estate for years, an estate for life, or an estate at will. It means "lease."

Demurrer

A legal objection made by one party to the opponent's pleading, alleging that it ought not be answered for some defect in law or the pleading.

Department of Real Estate

The state government agency that administers the provisions of the California Real Estate Law.

Department of Veterans Affairs

The current name of the federal government agency that administers GI or VA loans. Formerly known as the Veterans Administration or VA.

Deposit Receipt

A term used by the real estate industry to describe the written offer to purchase real property upon stated term and conditions, accompanied by a deposit toward the purchase price, which becomes the contract for the sale of the property upon acceptance by the owner.

Depreciation

Loss of value of property brought about by age, physical deterioration or functional or economic obsolescence. The term is also used in accounting to identify the amount of the decrease in value of an asset that is allowed in computing the value of the property for tax purposes.

Depth Table

A statistical table that may be used to estimate the value of the added depth of a lot.

Dereliction

Wearing away, also see *reliction*

Desist and Refrain Order

An order directing a person to stop from committing an act in violation of the Real Estate Law.

Deterioration

Loss of value due to wear and tear.

Determinable Fee

An estate which may end on the happening of an event that may or may not occur.

Development Method

An appraisal method used to value raw land. The appraiser locates improved comparable property with a known value, deducts the cost of the improvements, and arrives at the value of the raw land. The appraiser or investor estimates the gross sales of the developed lots, and deducts the costs of development and expenses. The remainder indicates the present worth of the land after discounting for the time involved.

Devise

A gift or disposal of real property by last will and Testament.

Devisee

One who receives a gift of real property by will.

Devisor

One who disposes of real property by will.

Directional Growth

The location or direction toward which the residential sections of a city are destined or determined to grow.

Disciplinary Action

Administrative procedure taken by the Real Estate Commissioner which could result in the revocation or suspension of a real estate license.

Discount

To sell a promissory note before maturity at a price less than the outstanding principal balance of the note at the time of sale. Also an amount deducted in advance by the lender from the nominal principal of a loan as part of the cost to the borrower of obtaining the loan.

Discount Points

The amount of money the borrower or seller must pay the lender to get a mortgage at a stated interest rate. This amount is equal to the difference between the principal balance on the note and the lesser amount which a purchaser of the note would pay the original lender for it under market conditions. A point equals one percent of the loan.

Discretionary Powers of Agency

Those powers conferred upon an agent by the principal which empower the agent in certain circumstances to make decisions based on the agent's own judgment.

Disintegration

The last stage of the life cycle of property value; the decline or decay stage.

Disintermediation

The relatively sudden withdrawal of substantial sums of money savers have deposited with savings and loan associations, commercial banks, and mutual savings banks. This term can also be considered to include life insurance policy purchasers borrowing against the value of their policies. The essence of this phenomenon is financial intermediaries losing within a short period of time billions of dollars as owners of funds held by those institutional lenders exercise their prerogative of taking them out of the hands of these financial institutions.

Disposable Income

The after-tax income a household receives to spend on personal consumption.

Dispossess

To deprive one of the use of real estate.

Distribution

An appraisal method used to establish land value separate from the improvements. The appraiser may observe that in a given area 20% of the sales price is land value or use the tax assessor's ratio and apply this percentage

to the appraised property. This is also called abstraction or allocation.

Doctrine of Relation Back

The title received by the successful bidder at a foreclosure sale relates back to the time when the borrower first signed the security. This causes certain intervening liens, except for some tax liens, to be cut off by the foreclosure sale.

Documentary Transfer Tax

A state enabling act allows a county to adopt a documentary transfer tax to apply on all transfers of real property located in the county. Notice of payment is entered on face of the deed or on a separate paper filed with the deed.

Documents

Legal instruments such as mortgages, contracts, deeds, options, wills, bills of sale, etc.

Dominant Tenement

The property benefiting by an easement appurtenant.

Donee

A person who receives a gift.

Donor

A person who makes a gift.

Double Declining Balance Depreciation

(See Declining Balance Depreciation.)

Draw

Usually applies to construction loans when disbursement of a portion of the mortgage is made in advance, as improvements to the property are made.

Dual Agency

An agency relationship in which the agent acts concurrently for both of the principals in a transaction.

Dual Agent

An agent who represents both sides in a

transaction at the same time. To be legal the knowledge and consent of all parties is required.

Due on Sale Clause

An acceleration clause granting the lender the right to demand full payment of the mortgage upon a sale of the property.

Due Process of Law

The principle that notice and an opportunity to be heard must be given the individuals affected when government powers are exercised.

Duress

Unlawful constraint exercised upon a person whereby he or she is forced to do some act against his or her will.

E

Earnest Money

Down payment made by a purchaser of real estate as evidence of good faith. A deposit or partial payment.

Easement

A right, privilege or interest limited to a specific purpose which one party has in the land of another.

Easement in Gross

An easement held by a person or an entity such as a public utility company not for the benefit of any specific land.

Economic Life

The period over which a property will yield a return on the investment over and above the economic or ground rent due to land.

Economic Obsolescence

A loss in value due to factors away from the subject property but adversely affecting the value of the subject property.

Economic Rent

The reasonable rental expectancy if the property were available for renting at the time of its valuation.

Effective Age of Improvement

The number of years of age that is indicated by the condition of the structure, distinct from chronological age.

Effective Date of Value

The specific day the conclusion of value applies.

Effective Gross Income

Gross income, less vacancy and bad debt allowance.

Effective Interest Rate

The percentage of interest that is actually being paid by the borrower for the use of the money, distinct from nominal interest.

Egress

A way to get out or exit. One of the purposes of an easement.

Ejectment

An action to recover possession of land that was wrongfully obtained.

Elevation

A drawing showing the exterior sides of a building as it will appear when completed. The type and placement of windows are detailed, as are other openings such as doors, dormers, vents and skylights.

Emancipated Minor

A person under the age of 18 who is married, divorced, serving in the armed forces or has received a declaration of emancipation by court order. Such a person has certain legal rights of an adult.

Emblements

Crops produced annually by the labor of the cultivator. The right of a tenant farmer to remove the annual crops he has produced after the tenancy has ended.

Eminent Domain

The right of the government to acquire property for necessary public or quasi-public use by condition; the owner must be fairly compensated and the right of the private citizen to get paid is spelled out in the 5th Amendment to the United States Constitution.

Employee

A person under control and supervision of the employer as distinguished from an independent contractor.

Encroachment

An unlawful intrusion onto another's adjacent property by improvements to real property, e.g. a swimming pool built across a property line.

Encumber

To voluntarily or involuntarily place a lien or charge on land or a limitation on the use of property.

Encumbrance

Anything which affects or limits the fee simple title to or value of property, e.g., mortgages or easements.

Endorsement

The act of signing one's name on the back of a check or /note, with or without further qualification.

Enforceable

A contract or agreement which the parties can be compelled to perform by a court of law or equity.

Equilibrium

The middle stage of the life cycle of property value. The equilibrium point is the static point at the peak of its value.

Equity

The interest or value which an owner has in real estate over and above the liens against it. Branch of remedial justice by and through which relief is afforded to suitors in courts of equity.

Equity Build-Up

The increase of owner's equity in property due to mortgage principal reduction and value appreciation.

Equity Participation

A mortgage transaction in which the lender, in addition to receiving a fixed rate of interest on the loan acquires an interest in the borrower's real property, and shares in the profits derived from the real property.

Equity of Redemption

The right to redeem property during the foreclosure period, such as a mortgagor's right to redeem within either 3 months or 1 year as may be permitted after foreclosure sale.

Erosion

The wearing away of land by the act of water, wind or glacial ice.

Escalation

The right reserved by the lender to increase the amount of the payments and/or interest upon the happening of a certain event.

Escalator Clause

A clause in a contract providing for the upward or downward adjustment of certain items to cover specified contingencies, usually tied to some index or event. Often used in long term leases to provide for rent adjustments, to cover tax and maintenance increases.

Escheat

The reverting of property to the State when heirs capable of inheriting are lacking.

Escrow

The deposit of instruments and/or funds with instructions with a third neutral party to carry out the provisions of an agreement or contract.

Escrow Agent

The neutral third party holding funds or something of value in trust for another or others.

Estate

As applied to real estate, the term signifies the quantity of interest, share, right, equity, of which riches or fortune may consist in real property. The degree, quantity, nature and extent of interest which a person has in real property.

Estate in Entirety

An estate held in many states by husband and wife together so long as both live and after the death of either by the survivor. Not used in California which is a community property state.

Estate in Fee

The most inclusive type of ownership of real property in perpetuity (forever) and inheritable (willable). This type of ownership is also called fee, fee simple estate, fee simple absolute estate or estate of inheritance.

Estate in Remainder

A future interest given by the grantor to a third person to take effect upon the termination of a life estate.

Estate in Reversion

The future interest retained by the grantor, for example to regain possession upon the termination of a leasehold or life estate.

Estate of Inheritance

An estate which may descend to heirs. All freehold estates are estates of inheritance, except estates for life.

Estate For Life

A possessory, freehold estate in land held by a person only for the duration of his or her life or the life or lives of another.

Estate From Period To Period

An interest in land where there is no definite termination date but the rental period is fixed at a certain sum per week, month, or year. Also called a periodic tenancy.

Estate At Sufferance

An estate arising when the tenant wrongfully holds over after the expiration of the term. The landlord has the choice of evicting the tenant as a trespasser or accepting such tenant for a similar term and under the conditions of the tenant's previous holding. Also called a tenancy at sufferance.

Estate At Will

The occupation of lands and tenements by a tenant for an indefinite period, terminable by one or both parties.

Estate For Years

An interest in lands by virtue of a contract for the possession of them for a definite and limited period of time. May be for a year or less. A lease may be said to be an estate for years.

Estimate

A preliminary opinion of value. Appraise, set a value.

Estimated Remaining Life

The period of time (years) it takes for the improvements to become valueless.

Estoppel

A legal theory under which a person is barred from asserting or denying a fact because of the person's previous acts or words.

Ethics

That branch of moral science, idealism, justness, and fairness, which treats of the duties which a member of a profession or craft owes to the public, client or partner, and to professional brethren or members. Accepted standards of right and wrong. Moral conduct, behavior or duty.

Et Ux

Abbreviation for "et uxor." Means "and wife."

Eviction

Dispossession by process of law. The act of depriving a person of the possession of lands in pursuance of the judgment of a court.

Exceptions

Matters affecting title to a particular parcel of real property which are included from coverage of a title insurance policy.

Exchange

A means of trading equities in two or more real properties, treated as a single transaction through a single escrow.

Exclusion

General matters affecting title to real property excluded from coverage of a title insurance policy.

Exclusive Agency Listing

A listing agreement employing a broker as the sole agent for the seller of real property under the terms of which the broker is entitled to a commission if the property is sold through any other broker, but not if a sale is negotiated by the owner without the services of an agent.

Exclusive Right To Sell Listing

A listing agreement employing a broker to act as agent for the seller of real property under the terms of which the broker is entitled to a commission if the property is sold during the duration of the listing through another broker or by the owner without the services of an agent.

Exculpatory

Excusing, clearing or tending to clear from alleged fault or responsibility.

Execute

To complete, to make, to perform, to do, to follow out; to execute a deed, to make a deed, including especially signing, sealing and delivery; to execute a contract is to perform the contract, to follow out to the end, to complete.

Executor

A man named in a will to carry out its provisions as to the disposition of the estate of a deceased person. (A woman is executrix.)

Executory Contract

A contract in which something remains to be done by one or both of the parties.

Executrix

A term sometimes used for a female executor.

Expenses

Certain items which appear on a closing statement in connection with a real estate sale.

Express

To state; to put into words or writing. "Express" is the opposite of implied.

Extended Coverage

A broad form of title insurance that is available to homeowners from the American Land Title Insurance Company (ALTA). It covers unrecorded liens and other matters not in the standard policy.

F

Facade

The front of a building, often used to refer to a false front and as a metaphor.

Fair Market Value.

This is the amount of money that would be paid for a property offered on the open market for a reasonable period of time with both buyer and seller knowing all the uses to which the property could be put and with neither party being under pressure to buy or sell.

Fannie Mae

An acronymic nickname for Federal National Mortgage Association (FNMA).

Farmers Home Administration

An agency of the Department of Agriculture. Primary responsibility is to provide financial assistance for farmers and others living in rural areas where financing is not available on reasonable terms from private sources.

Feasibility Study

An economic analysis of market data relating to a proposed project, including projected income and expenses, highest and best use, analysis of the economic base of the community, local zoning codes and other factors that might influence the feasibility of the project.

Federal Deposit Insurance Corporation

(FDIC) Agency of the federal government which insures deposits at commercial banks, savings banks and savings and loans.

Federal Home Loan Bank

A federal organization formed in 1932 to provide a credit reserve system for savings and loan associations from which they are able to borrow funds for short or long terms.

Federal Home Loan Mortgage Corporation

An independent stock company which creates a secondary market in conventional residential loans and in FHA and VA loans by purchasing mortgages.

Federal Housing Administration

(FHA) An agency of the federal government that insures private mortgage loans for financing of new and existing homes and home repairs.

Federal Land Bank System

Federal government agency making long term loans to farmers.

Federal National Mortgage Association

(FNMA) "Fannie Mae" a quasi public agency converted into a private corporation whose primary function is to buy and sell FHA and VA mortgages in the secondary market.

Federal Reserve System

The federal banking system of the United States under the control of central board of governors (Federal Reserve Board) involving a central bank in each of twelve geographical districts with broad powers in controlling credit and the amount of money in circulation.

Fee

An estate of inheritance in real property.

Fee Simple Absolute

Ownership of real property in perpetuity (forever), without time limit or end. It is the greatest and most inclusive type of real estate ownership; also called "fee" and an estate of inheritance.

Fee Simple Defeasible

An estate in fee subject to the occurrence of a condition subsequent whereby the estate may be terminated.

Fee Simple Estate

The greatest interest that one can have in real property. An estate that is unqualified, of indefinite duration, freely transferable and inheritable.

Felony

A major crime for which the penalty is usually imprisonment in a penitentiary. Conviction of some felonies can impair a person's capacity to enter into a valid contract.

Feudal Tenure

A real property ownership system in which ownership rests with a sovereign who may grant lesser interests in return for service or loyalty. This is in contrast to allodial tenure.

FHA

The Federal Housing Administration, the federal government agency that *insures* private mortgages. Such loans are called *FHA* insured loans.

FHLMC

See Federal Home Loan Mortgage Corporation.

Fictitious Deed of Trust

A recorded generic deed of trust that does not relate to a specific transaction and is used for reference in short-form deeds of trust.

Fictitious Name

A name used for business purposes that is not the true name of the owner. Also called "*DBA*," for "doing business as."

Fidelity Bond

A security posted for the discharge of an obligation of personal services.

Fiduciary

A person in a position of trust and confidence, as between principal and broker; broker as fiduciary owes certain loyalty which cannot be breached under the rules of agency.

Fiduciary Duty

That duty owed by an agent to act in the highest good faith toward the principal and not to obtain any advantage over the latter by the slightest misrepresentation, concealment, duress or pressure.

Filtering

The process whereby higher-priced properties become available to lower income buyers.

Financial Intermediary

Financial institutions such as commercial banks, savings and loan associations, mutual savings banks and life insurance companies which receive relatively small sums of money from the public and invest them in the form of large sums. A considerable portion of these funds are loaned on real estate.

Financing Process

The systematic 5 step procedure followed by major institutional lenders in analyzing a proposed loan, which includes filing of application by a borrower; lender's analysis of borrower and property; processing of loan documentation; closing (paying) the loan; and servicing (collection and record keeping).

Financing Statement

The instrument which is filed in order to give public notice of the security interest and thereby protect the interest of the secured parties in the collateral. (See definition of Security Interest and Secured Party.)

First Mortgage

A legal document pledging collateral 'for a loan (See "mortgage") that has first priority over all other claims against the property except taxes and bonded indebtedness. That mortgage superior to any other.

First Trust Deed

A legal document pledging collateral for a loan (See "trust deed") that has first priority over all other claims against the property except taxes and bonded indebtedness. That trust deed superior to any other.

Fiscal Controls

Federal tax revenue and expenditure policies used to control the level of economic activity.

Fiscal Year

A business or accounting year as distinguished from a calendar year.

Fixed Expenses

The regular recurring costs required in owning a property such as taxes and fire insurance.

Fixity of Location

The physical characteristic of real estate that subjects it to the influence of its surroundings.

Fixtures

Appurtenances attached to the land or improvements, which usually cannot be removed without agreement as they become real property; examples are plumbing fixtures, store fixtures built into the property, etc.

Flat Lease

A lease in which the rent is a fixed sum paid periodically throughout the entire lease term.

Flood Waters

Waters overflowing a regularly defined channel.

Floor Plan

A plan drawn to scale indicating wall-to- wall dimensions, room sizes and exposures and the placements of windows, doors, partitions, etc.

FNMA

Federal National Mortgage Association, called *Fannie Mae*. Formerly a federally-related agency, it is now a private corporation that buys and sells mortgages in the secondary market.

Forecasting

Projection of the future by taking the past and present as a guide and tempered with the appraiser's judgment.

Foreclosure

Procedure whereby property pledged as security for a debt is sold to pay the debt in event of default in payments or terms.

Forfeiture

Loss of money or anything of value, due to failure to perform.

Foundation Plan

A scale drawing showing the size of footings, size and dimensions of piers and the construction measurements and details of the sub- floor area.

Four-Three-Two-One Rule

An appraisal rule for computing depth factors of lots primarily in retail environments.

Franchise

A specified privilege awarded by a government or business firm which awards an exclusive dealership.

Fraud

The intentional and successful employment of any cunning, deception, collusion, or artifice, used to circumvent, cheat or deceive another person whereby that person acts upon it to the loss of property and to legal injury. (Actual Fraud is a deliberate misrepresentation or representation made in reckless disregard of its truth or its falsity, the suppression of truth, a promise made without the intention to perform it, or any other act intended to deceive.)

Frauds, Statute of

(See Statute of Frauds.)

"Freddie Mac"

(See Federal Home Loan Mortgage Corporation.)

Free and Clear

Encumbered by no liens and with no clouds on title.

Freehold Estate

An estate of indeterminable duration, e.g., fee simple or life estate.

Frontage

A term used to describe or identify that part of a parcel of land or an improvement on the land which faces a street. The term is also used to refer to the lineal extent of the land or improvement that is parallel to and facing the street, e.g., a 75-foot frontage.

Front Foot

Property measurement for sale or valuation purposes; the property measured by the front linear foot on its street line-each front foot extending the depth of the lot.

Front Money

The minimum amount of money necessary to initiate a real estate venture, to get the transaction underway.

Frostline

The depth of frost penetration in the soil. Varies in different parts of the country. Footings should be placed below this depth to prevent movement.

Fully Indexed Note Rate

As related to adjustable rate mortgages, the index value at the time of application plus the gross margin stated in the note.

Functional Obsolescence

A loss of value due to adverse factors from within the structure which affect the utility of the structure, value and marketability.

Future Benefits

The anticipated benefits the present owner will receive from the property in the future.

G

Gable Roof

A pitched roof with sloping sides. GAIN

A profit, benefit, or value increase.

Gambrel Roof

A curb roof, having a steep lower slope with a flatter upper slope above.

General Lien

A lien on all the property of a debtor.

General Liquor License

A license issued by the Department of Alcoholic Beverage Control (ABC) that authorizes the holder to engage in the sale of distilled spirits, wine and beer.

Gift Deed

A deed for which there is no consideration.

GI Loan

A guaranteed loan available to veterans under a federal government program administered by the Department of Veterans Affairs. It is also called a VA loan.

Goodwill

An intangible but salable asset of a business derived from the expectation of continued public patronage.

Government National Mortgage Association

An agency of HUD, which functions in the secondary mortgage market, primarily in social housing programs. Commonly called by the nickname "Ginnie Mae" (GNMA).

Government Survey

A method of specifying the location of parcel of land using prime meridians, base lines, standard parallels, guide meridians, townships and sections.

Grade

Ground level at the foundation.

Graduated Lease

Lease which provides for a varying rental rate, often based upon future determination; sometimes rent is based upon result of periodical appraisals; used largely in long-term leases.

Graduated Payment Mortgage

Providing for partially deferred payments of principal at start of loan. (There are a variety of plans.) Usually after the first five years of the loan term the principal and interest payment are substantially higher, to make up principal portion of payments lost at the beginning of the Loan. (See Variable Interest Rate.)

Grant

A technical legal term in a deed of conveyance bestowing an interest in real property on another. The words "convey" and "transfer" have the same effect.

Grant Deed

A limited warranty deed using the word "grant" or like words that assures a grantee that the grantor has not already conveyed the land to another and that the estate is free from encumbrances placed by the grantor.

Grantee

A person to whom a grant is made.

Grantor

A person who transfers his or her interest in property to another by grant.

Gratuitous Agent

A person not paid by the principal for services on behalf of the principal, who cannot be forced to act as an agent, but who becomes bound to act in good faith and obey a principal's instructions once he or she undertakes to act as an agent.

Grid

A chart used in rating the borrower risk, property and the neighborhood.

Gross Annual Multiplier

A factor (number) used to arrive at an estimate of value from the relationship between and by dividing the gross *annual* income (rent) into the selling or asking price of properties. Used for smaller commercial properties.

Gross Income

Total income from property before any expenses are deducted.

Gross Lease

A lease in which the lessee (tenant) pays an agreed rent and the lessor (owner) pays the expenses.

Gross Margin

With regard to an adjustable rate mortgage, an amount expressed as percentage points, stated in the note which is added to the current index value on the rate adjustment date to establish the new note rate.

Gross National Product (GNP)

The total value of all goods and services produced in an economy during a given period of time.

Gross Profit

Profit expressed as a percentage of selling price.

Gross Rate

A method of collecting interest by adding total interest to the principal of the loan at the outset of the term.

Gross Rent Multiplier

A number which, times the gross income of a property, produces an estimate of value of the property. Example The gross income from an unfurnished apartment building is $200,000 per annum. If an appraiser uses a gross multiplier of 7%, then it is said that based on the gross multiplier the value of the building is $1,400,000.

Ground Lease

An agreement for the use of the land only, sometimes secured by improvements placed on the land by the user.

Ground Rent

Earnings of improved property credited to earnings of the ground itself after allowance is made for earnings of improvements; often termed economic rent.

Guarantee of Title

A guarantee by a title company or abstract company that the title is vested as shown on the guarantee. The guarantee is backed only by the assets or reserves of the guarantor.

Guaranteed Inventory

A guarantee given by the seller of a business opportunity that the actual amount of inventory on hand at the close of escrow will equal the value placed upon the inventory at the time the sales agreement was entered into.

Guardian

One lawfully vested with the power and duty to care for and manage the affairs of a person who is unable to do so for himself.

H

Habendum Clause

The "to have and to hold" clause which may be found in a deed.

Habitability

Fit to live in according to the interpretations of the courts. Broader than tenantability which complies with the Civil Code.

Hard Money

Cash including the cash proceeds from a loan as distinguished from credit extended by a seller.

HB&M

The abbreviation for Humboldt Base and Meridian.

Heir

One who inherits property at the death of the owner of the land, if the owner has died without a will.

Hereditament

Anything capable of being inherited.

Highest And Best Use

An appraisal phrase meaning that use which at the time of an appraisal is most likely to produce the greatest net return to the land and/or buildings over a given period of time; that use which will produce the greatest amount of amenities or profit. This is the starting point for appraisal.

Hip Roof

A pitched roof with sloping sides and ends.

Historical Age

The actual age in years from the date a building was constructed. It is the same as *chronological age*, and may differ from "*effective age*."

Holder In Due Course

One who has taken a note, check or bill of exchange in due course: 1. before it was overdue; 2. in good faith and for value; and 3. without knowledge that it has been previously dishonored and without notice of any defect at the time it was negotiated to him or her.

Holdover Tenant

Tenant who remains in possession of leased property after the expiration of the lease term.

Holographic Will

A will that is written, dated and signed in the handwriting of the testator (maker). It need not be witnessed.

Homeowners Association

An organized group of homeowners whose members regulate and enforce the rules and standards of their community.

Homestead

(exemption) A statutory protection of real property used as a home from the claims of certain creditors and judgments up to a specified amount.

Hoskold Method Sinking Fund

An formula used in appraisal that is used to estimate the today's value of a series of annual payments of one dollar after discounting for loss of interest on each dollar to the time of its collection. The method condominium associations usually use to determine the annual reserve contribution.

Housing Financial Discrimination Act of 1977 (Holden Act)

California Health and Safety Code Section 35800, et seq., designed primarily to eliminate discrimination in lending practices based upon the character of the neighborhood in which real property is located. (See Redlining.)

HUD

The Department of Housing and Urban Development which is responsible for the implementation and administration of U.S. government housing and urban development programs.

Hundred Percent Location

A city retail business location which is considered the best available for attracting business.

Hypothecate

To pledge a thing as security without the necessity of giving up possession of it.

I

Illegal

An act contrary to law; in violation of the law.

Illusory

Deceptive; deceiving by false appearances or illusions.

ILSFDA

The Interstate Land Sales Full Disclosure Act is a federal law to control the sale of *large unimproved residential subdivisions in interstate commerce*.

Imperative Necessity

Circumstances under which an agent has expanded authority in an emergency, including the power to disobey instructions where it is clearly in the interests of the principal and where there is no time to obtain instructions from the principal.

Implied

Suggested, presumed, assumed, the opposite of *expressly stated in words*.

Impounds

A trust type account established by lenders for the accumulation of borrowers funds to meet periodic payment of taxes, FHA mortgage insurance premiums, and/or future insurance policy premiums, required to protect their security. Impounds are usually collected with the note payment. The combined principal, interest, taxes and insurance payment is commonly termed a PITI payment.

Income (Capitalization) Approach

One of the three methods of the appraisal process generally applied to income producing property, and involves a three-step process- (1) find net annual income, (2) set an appropriate capitalization rate or "present worth" factor, and (3) capitalize the income dividing the net income by the capitalization rate.

Improved Value

The combined value of land and building as distinguished from their separate values.

Imputed Notice

Information charged to a person as to a given fact affecting his or her rights on the grounds that actual notice *was given to some person* (their agent) whose duty it was to report the information to the person affected.

In the Business

A term used in connection with transactions in notes and sales contracts. Anyone who acquires for resale to the public and not as an investment, eight or more trust deeds or land contracts during one calendar year is considered to be "*in the business*," and is required to have a real estate *broker's license*.

Including Interest

A term for loan payments that includes both principal and interest – a level-payment plan or an amortized loan.

Incompetent

One who is mentally incompetent, incapable; any person who, though not insane, is, by reason of old age, disease, weakness of mind, or any other cause, unable, unassisted, to properly manage and take care of self or property and by reason thereof would be likely to be deceived or imposed upon by artful or designing persons.

Incorporeal Rights

Nonpossessory rights in real estate, a rising out of ownership, such as rents.

Increasing and Diminishing Returns

An appraisal principle that holds that as successively greater increments of land, labor or *capital* are applied to a property a greater or lesser yield is produced.

Increment

An increase. Most frequently used to refer to the increase of value of land that accompanies population growth and increasing wealth in the community. The term "unearned increment" is used in this connection since values are supposed to have increased without effort on the part of the owner.

Incurable Depreciation

Physical deterioration, functional obsolescence, or economic obsolescence that is physically impossible or economically impracticable to correct at this given time.

Indemnify

To take on liability and agree to compensate someone for any hurt, loss or damage suffered by them.

Indemnity Agreement

An agreement by the maker of the document to repay the addressee of the agreement up to the limit stated for any loss due to the contingency stated on the agreement.

Indenture

A formal written instrument made between two or more persons in different interests, such as a lease.

Independent Contractor

A person who acts for another but who sells final results and whose methods of achieving those results are not subject to the control of another.

Ingress

A way in or an entrance. It can be a purpose of an easement.

Inherit

To receive property by the laws of inheritance and not by a will.

Initial Note Rate

With regard to an adjustable rate mortgage, the note rate upon origination. This rate may differ from the fully indexed note rate.

Initial Rate Discount

As applies to an adjustable rate mortgage, the index value at the time of loan application plus the margin less the initial note rate.

Injunction

A writ or order issued under the seal of a court to restrain one or more parties to a suit or proceeding from doing an act which is deemed to be inequitable or unjust in regard to the rights of some other party or parties in the suit or proceeding.

Installment Loan

A loan providing for payment of the principal in two or more payments at different stated times.

Installment Note

A note which provides for a series of periodic payments of principal and interest, until amount borrowed is paid in full. This periodic reduction of principal amortizes the loan.

Installment Reporting

A method of reporting capital gains by installments for successive tax years to minimize the impact of the totality of the capital gains tax in the year of the sale.

Installment Sale

A sale that permits the taxpayer to prorate the tax on the capital gain over the term of the installment contract, provided at least one payment is received after the tax year in which the sale occurs.

Installment Sales Contract

Commonly called contract of sale or "land contract." Purchase of real estate wherein the purchase price is paid in installments over a long period of time, title is retained by seller, and upon default by buyer (vendee) the payments may be forfeited.

Institutional Lenders

A financial intermediary or depository, such as a savings and loan association, commercial bank, or life insurance company, which pools money of its depositors and then invests funds in various ways, including trust deed and mortgage loans.

Instrument

A written legal document; created to effect the rights of the parties, giving formal expression to a legal act or agreement for the purpose of creating, modifying or terminating a right. Real estate lenders' basic instruments are promissory notes, deeds of trust, mortgages, installment sales contracts, leases, assignments.

Intangible

Property that cannot be touched such as *goodwill*.

Integration

The initial stage of the life cycle of property value, the development stage.

Interest

A portion, share or right in something. Partial, not complete ownership. The charge in dollars for the use of money for a period of time. In a sense, the "rent" paid for the use of money.

Interest Extra Loan

A loan in which a fixed amount of principal is repaid in installments along with interest accrued each period on the amount of the then outstanding principal only.

Interest Only Loan

A straight, non-amortizing loan in which the lender receives only interest during the term of the loan and principal is repaid in a lump sum at maturity.

Interest Rate

The percentage of a sum of money charged for its use. Rent or charge paid for use of money, expressed as a percentage per month or year of the sum borrowed.

Interim Financing

A loan used to finance construction, due at the completion of the construction and usually paid off with the proceeds of a "take out" loan.

Interim Loan

A short-term, temporary loan used until permanent financing is available, e.g., a construction loan.

Intermediation

The process of pooling and supplying funds for investment by financial institutions called intermediaries. The process is dependent on individual savers placing their funds with these institutions and foregoing opportunities to directly invest in the investments selected.

Interpleader

A court proceeding initiated by the stakeholder of property who claims no proprietary interest in it for the purpose of deciding who among claimants is legally entitled to the property.

Interval Ownership

A form of timeshare ownership. (See Timeshare Ownership.)

Intestate

A person who dies having made no will, or one which is defective in form, is said to have died intestate, in which case the estate descends to the heirs at law or next of kin.

Inventory

A detailed list of the stock-in-trade of a business.

Inverse Condemnation

A lawsuit by an owner to obtain just compensation from a governmental authority when the owner's property has been substantially impaired or effectively taken by the authority.

Involuntary Lien

A lien imposed against property without consent of an owner; example taxes, special assessments, federal income tax liens, etc.

Inwood Compound Interest Method

An appraisal formula used to estimate the value as of today of a series of annual payments of principal and interest of one dollar.

Irrevocable

Incapable of being recalled or revoked, unchangeable.

Irrigation Districts

Quasi-political districts created under special laws to provide for water services to property owners in the district; an operation governed to a great extent by law.

J

Joint Note

A note signed by two or more persons who have equal liability for payment.

Joint Tenancy   *ττιρ*

Undivided ownership of a property interest by two or more persons each of whom has a right to an equal share in the interest and a right of survivorship, i.e., the right to share equally with other surviving joint tenants in the interest of a deceased joint tenant.

Joint Venture

Two or more individuals or firms joining together on a single project as partners.

Jointly and Severally Liable

Each party may be sued individually for the entire amount on a note or *all parties* may be sued together.

Judgment

The final determination of a court of competent jurisdiction of a matter presented to it; money judgments provide for the payment of claims presented to the court, or are awarded as damages, etc.

Judgment Lien

A legal claim on all of the property of a judgment debtor which enables the judgment creditor to have the property sold for payment of the amount of the judgment.

Judicial Foreclosure

A sale of property by a court to satisfy a debt.

Junior Mortgage

A mortgage recorded subsequently to another mortgage on the same property or made subordinate by agreement to a later-recorded mortgage.

Jurisdiction

The authority by which judicial officers take cognizance of and decide causes; the power to hear and determine a cause; the right and power which a judicial officer has to enter upon the inquiry.

K

Key Lot

A lot so located that the rear adjoins one side of other lots. Usually considered the least desirable lot in a subdivision.

Kiosk

A small, light structure with one or more open sides often seen in shopping centers as a photo shop, key shop or newsstand.

L

Laches

Delay or negligence in asserting one's legal rights.

Land

The material of the earth, whatever may be the ingredients of which it is composed, whether soil, rock, or other substance, and includes free or unoccupied space for an indefinite distance upwards as well as downwards.

Land Contract

A contract used in a sale of real property whereby the seller retains title to the property until all or a prescribed part of the purchase price has been paid. Also commonly called a conditional sales contract, installment sales contract or real property sales contract. (See Real Property Sales Contract for statutory definition.)

Land and Improvement Loan

A loan obtained by the builder/developer for the purchase of land and to cover expenses for subdividing.

Landlord

One who rents his or her property to another. The lessor under a lease.

Land Project

Defined by the Subdivided Lands Act as a subdivision containing 50 or more unimproved parcels for residential use, located in a sparsely populated area.

Land Residual Technique

An appraisal method in the income approach of estimating the value of the land as separate from the building.

Late Charge

A charge assessed by a lender against a borrower failing to make loan installment payments when due.

Later Date Order

The commitment for an owner's title insurance policy issued by a title insurance company which covers the seller's title as of the date of the contract. When the sale closes the purchaser orders the title company to record the deed to purchaser and bring down their examination to cover this later date so as to show purchaser as owner of the property.

Lateral Support

The support which the soil of an adjoining owner gives to a neighbor's land.

Lawful Object

An object of a contract that is permitted by law and possible of performance.

Lease

A contract between owner and tenant, setting forth conditions upon which tenant may occupy and use the property and the term of the occupancy. Sometimes used as an alternative to purchasing property outright, as a method of financing right to occupy and use real property.

Leasehold Estate

A tenant's right to occupy real estate during the term of the lease. This is a personal property interest.

Legacy

A gift of personal property, usually money, by will.

Legal

Permitted or required by law; conforming to the law.

Legal Description

A land description recognized by law; a description by which property can be definitely located by reference to government surveys or approved recorded maps.

Legal Person

A legal entity, usually a corporation, having certain powers and duties of a natural person.

Legal Rate

An interest rate fixed by statute for cases where it has not been fixed by contract.

Legatee

A receiver of personal property by will.

Lessee

One who contracts to rent, occupy, and use property under a lease agreement; a tenant.

Lessor

An owner who enters into a lease agreement with a tenant; a landlord.

Less Than Freehold

An estate that is limited in time or by the desire of the parties such as with a leasehold. Having the capability to theoretically determine the ending date on a calendar.

Level-Payment Mortgage

A loan on real estate that is paid off by making a series of equal (or nearly equal) regular payments. Part of the payment is usually interest on the loan and part of it reduces the amount of the unpaid principal balance of the loan. Also sometimes called an "amortized mortgage" or "installment mortgage."

Leverage

The use of debt financing of an investment to maximize the return per dollar of equity invested.

Liabilities

Claims of creditors or debts.

License

An authorization by law to do some specific thing, such as to enter upon the land of another for a particular purpose or to practice a profession.

Lien

A form of encumbrance which usually makes specific property security for the payment of a debt or discharge of an obligation. Example - judgments, taxes, mortgages, deeds of trust, etc.

Life Estate

An estate or interest in real property, which is held for the duration of the life of some certain person. It may be limited by the life of the person holding it or by the life of some other person.

Life Of Loan Cap (Cap Rate)

With regard to an adjustable rate mortgage, a ceiling the note rate cannot exceed over the life of the loan.

Limitations, Statute of

The commonly used identifying term for various statutes which require that a legal action be commenced within a prescribed time after the accrual of the right to seek legal relief.

Limited Partnership

A partnership consisting of a general partner or partners and limited partners in which the general partners manage and control the business affairs of the partnership while limited partners are essentially investors taking no part in the management of the partnership and having no liability for the debts of the partnership in excess of their invested capital.

Lintel

A horizontal board that supports the load over an opening such as a door or window.

Liquidated Damages

A sum agreed upon by the parties to be full damages if a certain event occurs.

Liquidated Damages Clause

A clause in a contract by which the parties by agreement fix the damages in advance for a breach of the contract.

Liquidity

Holdings in or the ability to convert assets to cash or its equivalent. The ease with which a person is able to pay maturing obligations.

Lis Pendens

A notice filed or recorded for the purpose of warning all persons that the title or right to the possession of certain real property is in litigation; literally "suit pending;" usually recorded so as to give constructive notice of pending litigation.

Listing

An employment contract between principal and agent authorizing the agent to perform services for the principal involving the latter's property; listing contracts are entered into for the purpose of securing persons to buy, lease, or rent property. Employment of an agent by a prospective purchaser or lessee to locate property for purchase or lease may be considered a listing.

Listing Agent

The real estate broker who has obtained a listing.

Littoral

Land bordering a *lake* the sea or other body of water other than in a watercourse.

Livery Of Seisin (Seizin)

The appropriate ceremony at common law for transferring the possession of lands by a grantor to a grantee.

Loan Administration

Also called loan servicing Mortgage bankers not only originate loans, but also "service" them from origination to maturity of the loan through handling of loan payments, delinquencies, impounds, payoffs and releases.

Loan Application

The loan application is a source of information on which the lender bases a decision to make the loan; defines the terms of the loan contract, gives the name of the borrower, place of employment, salary, bank accounts, and credit references, and describes the real estate that is to be mortgaged. It also stipulates the amount of loan being applied for and repayment terms.

Loan Closing

When all conditions have been met, the loan officer authorizes the recording of the trust deed or mortgage. The dispersal procedure of funds is similar to the closing of a real estate sales escrow. The borrower can expect to receive less than the amount of the loan, as title, recording, service, and other fees may be withheld, or can expect to deposit the cost of these items into the loan escrow. This process is sometimes called "funding" the loan.

Loan Commitment

Lender's contractual commitment to make a loan based on the appraisal and underwriting.

Loan Correspondent

A representative who negotiates or services loans for a lender.

Loan-To-Value Ratio

The percentage of a property's value that a lender can or may loan to a borrower. For example, if the ratio is 80% this means that a lender may loan 80% of the property's appraised value to a borrower.

Loan Listing

An agency contract in which the agent is finding a lender for a borrower. It can not legally exceed 45 days.

Loan Origination Fee

A fee charged by a lender for setting up the loan records and file. It is a fee for services, not interest and therefore is not deductible for income tax purposes but it is considered as part of the finance charge under Regulation Z and is included in the Annual Percentage Rate.

Loan Value

The value usually established by an appraiser for a lender for the purpose of determining the amount of a new trust deed or mortgage. It is usually a percentage of the market value.

Lock-in

A clause that may appear in a note prohibiting the buyer from paying off the indebtedness early.

Long-term Capital Gain

Gain or profit on the sale of property owned for more than one year. The maximum tax rate on long-term capital gain is lower than the maximum rate on ordinary income.

Lot Split

The division of an existing small parcel into two separate parcels.

M

MAI

Member of the Appraisal Institute. Designates a person who is a member of the American Institute of Real Estate Appraisers.

Margin Of Security

The difference between the amount of the mortgage loan (s) and the appraised value of the property.

Marginal Land

Land which barely pays the cost of working or using.

Market Data Approach

One of the three methods in the appraisal process. A means of comparing similar type properties, which have recently sold, to the subject property. Commonly used in comparing residential properties.

Market Price

The price paid regardless of pressures, motives or intelligence.

Market Value

The highest price in terms of money which a property will bring in a competitive and open market and under all conditions required for a fair sale, i.e., the buyer and seller acting prudently, knowledgeably and neither affected by undue pressures.

Marketable Title

Title which a reasonable purchaser, informed as to the facts and their legal importance and acting with reasonable care, would be willing and ought to accept.

Material Change of Ownership

Sale of five or more parcels to one buyer by a subdivider.

Material Fact

A fact is material if it is one which the agent should realize would be likely to affect the judgment of the principal in giving his or her consent to the agent to enter into the particular transaction on the specified terms.

MDB&M

The abbreviation for Mount Diablo Base and Meridian.

Mechanic's Lien

A lien created by statute which exists against real property in favor of persons who have performed work or furnished materials for the improvement of the real property.

Megalopolis

An extensive, heavily-populated, continuously urban area, including any number of cities.

Merger

The union of two or more separate interests by the transfer of all the interests into one, for example, the acquisition of an adjacent parcel.

Meridians

Imaginary north-south lines which intersect base lines to form a starting point for the measurement of land.

Mesne Profits

Profit from land use accruing between two periods as for example moneys owed to the owner of land by a person who has illegally occupied the land after the owner takes title, but before taking possession.

Metes And Bounds

A term used in describing the boundary lines of land, setting forth all the boundary lines together with their terminal points and angles. Metes (length or measurements) and Bounds (boundaries) description is often used when a great deal of accuracy is required.

Mile

5,280 feet.

Mill

One-tenth of a cent, a unit used in real property tax rates.

Minimum Property Requirements

abbreviated MPR. Minimum standards of planning, construction, and general acceptability required on FHA loans for the purchase or construction of residential property.

Minor

A person under 18 years of age.

Misplaced Improvements

Improvements on land which do not conform to the most profitable use of the site.

Misrepresentation

A false or misleading statement or assertion.

Mobilehome

As defined in Business and Professions Code Section 10131.6(c), "mobilehome" means a structure transportable in one or more sections, designed and equipped to contain not more than two dwelling units to be used with or without a foundation system. "Mobilehome" does not include a recreational vehicle, as defined in Section 18010.5 of the Health and Safety Code, a commercial coach, as defined in Section 18012 of the Health and Safety Code, or factory-built housing, as defined in Section 19971 of the Health and Safety Code.

Modernization

Bringing a property into conformity with changes in style, whether interior or exterior.

Modular

A system for the construction of dwellings and other improvements to real property through the on-site assembly of component parts (modules) that have been mass produced away from the building site.

Moldings

Usually patterned strips used to provide ornamental variation of outline or contour, such as cornices, bases, window and door jambs.

Monetary Controls

Federal Reserve tools for regulating the availability of money and credit to influence the level of economic activity, such as adjusting discount rates, reserve requirements, etc.

Month-to-Month Tenancy

A lease of real property for the term of one month, renewable for each succeeding month at the option of either party. Technically called an estate of periodic tenancy.

Monument

A fixed object and point established by surveyors to establish land locations.

Moratorium

The temporary suspension, usually by statute, of the enforcement of liability of debt. Temporary suspension of development or utilities connections imposed by local government.

Mortgage

An instrument recognized by law by which property is hypothecated to secure the payment of a debt or obligation; a procedure for foreclosure in event of default is established by statute.

Mortgage Banker

A person whose principal business is the originating, financing, closing, selling and servicing of loans secured by real property for institutional lenders on a contractual basis.

Mortgage Company

A mortgage banker or mortgage broker.

Mortgage Contracts With Warrants

Warrants make the mortgage more attractive to the lender by providing both the greater security that goes with a mortgage, and the opportunity of a greater return through the right to buy either stock in the borrower's company or a portion of the income property itself.

Mortgage Guaranty Insurance

Insurance against financial loss available to mortgage lenders from private mortgage insurance companies (PMICs).

Mortgage Investment Company

A company or group of private investors that buys mortgages for investment purposes.

Mortgage Loan Disclosure Statement

The statement on a form approved by the Real Estate Commissioner which is required by law to be furnished by a mortgage loan broker to the prospective borrower of loans of a statutorily- prescribed amount before the borrower becomes obligated to complete the loan.

Mortgagee

One to whom a mortgagor gives a mortgage to secure a loan or performance of an obligation; a lender or creditor. (See definition of secured party.)

Mortgagor

One who gives a mortgage on his or her property to secure a loan or assure performance of an obligation; a borrower.

Multiple Listing

A listing, usually an exclusive right to sell, taken by a member of an organization composed of real estate brokers, with the provisions that all members will have the opportunity to find an interested buyer; a cooperative listing insuring owner property will receive a wider market exposure.

Multiple Listing Service

An association of real estate agents providing for a pooling of listings and the sharing of commissions on a specified basis.

Mutual Consent

Approval or assent by both parties to the terms of a contract. Consent is one of the four essential elements to have a valid contract and it is achieved by offer, acceptance and communication.

Mutual Mortgage Insurance

A type of FHA insurance, abbreviated MMI. The premium is collected by the lender, often by adding it to the loan and paid to the FHA. This fund insures lenders against loss and provides funds for the full operation of the FHA.

Mutual Savings Banks

Financial institutions owned by depositors each of whom has rights to net earnings of the bank in proportion to his or her deposits.

Mutual Water Company

A water company organized by or for water users in a given district with the object of securing an ample water supply at a reasonable rate; stock is issued to users.

N

Narrative Appraisal

A summary of all factual materials, techniques and appraisal methods used by the appraiser in setting forth his or her value conclusion.

Natural Person

A living person, as distinguished from a legal person or corporation.

Negative Amortization

Occurs when monthly installment payments are insufficient to pay the interest accruing on the principal balance, so that the unpaid interest must be added to the principal due.

Negative Fraud

The withholding of a material fact from another party which induces them to enter into a contract that causes them damage or loss.

Negotiable

Capable of being negotiated, assignable or transferable in the ordinary course of business.

Negotiable Instrument

A promissory note or check that meets certain legal requirements that allows it to be traded freely in commerce.

Neighborhood

An area of similar buildings, occupants or business enterprises within a larger community.

Net Income

The money remaining after expenses are deducted from income; the profit.

Net Operating Income

The anticipated net income after deducting all operating expenses from effective gross income but before deducting debt service or income taxes. Effective Gross Income less Operating Expense equals NOI.

Net Lease

A lease requiring a lessee to pay charges against the property such as taxes, insurance and maintenance costs in addition to rental payments.

Net Listing

A listing which provides that the agent may retain as compensation for agent's services all sums received over and above a net price to the owner.

Net Profit

Profit expressed as a percentage of cost.

Net Spendable

The cash remaining from gross income after deducting operating expenses, principal and interest payments and income taxes. It is also called spendable income.

Net Worth

The difference between assets and liabilities or an *owner's equity* in a business.

Nominal Interest Rates

The percentage of interest that is stated in loan documents.

Non-institutional Lender

A source of real estate loan funds other than a bank or similar institution, such as mortgage companies, pension funds, individuals and finance companies.

Notary Public

An appointed officer with authority to take the acknowledgment of persons executing documents, sign the certificate, and affix official seal.

Note

A signed written instrument acknowledging a debt and promising payment, according to the specified terms and conditions. A promissory note.

Note Rate

This rate determines the amount of interest charged on an annual basis to the borrower. Also called the "accrual rate", "contract rate" or "coupon rate."

Notice

(1) Actual notice: Express or implied knowledge of a fact. (2) Constructive notice: A fact, imputed to a person by law, which should have been discovered because of the person's actual notice of circumstances and the inquiry that a prudent person would have been expected to make. (3) Legal Notice: Information required to be given by law.

Notice of Abandonment

The document recorded to terminate a Homestead.

Notice of Cessation

A notice filed by an owner after work has ceased on a construction project thereby limiting the time in which to file a Mechanic's Lien to 60 days for the original contractor and 30 days for all other (sub) contractors.

Notice of Completion

A notice recorded by the party who ordered work or improvements, placing time limits for recording Mechanic's Liens.

Notice of Intention to Sell

A document that is recorded and published prior to the sale of a business opportunity in order to give notice to the seller's creditors. It is also called Notice to Creditors of Bulk Transfer.

Notice of Intention to Transfer

A document that must be recorded and filed with the Department of Alcoholic Beverage Control prior to transfer of a liquor license.

Notice of Nonresponsibility

A notice provided by law designed to relieve property owner from responsibility for the cost of unauthorized work done on the property or materials furnished therefor; notice must be verified, recorded and posted.

Notice To Quit

A notice to a tenant to vacate rented property.

Novation

The substitution or exchange of a new obligation or contract for an old one by the mutual agreement of the parties.

Null and Void

Of no legal validity or effect.

Nuncupative Will

An oral will made in contemplation of death no longer recognized in California law.

O

Obligatory Advances

Disbursements of money which the lender under the terms of a loan is bound to make over the period of the construction loan.

Obsolescence

Loss in value due to reduced desirability and usefulness of a structure because its design and construction become obsolete; loss because of becoming antiquated and not in keeping with modern needs, with resultant loss of income. May be functional or economic.

Offer To Purchase

The proposal made to an owner of property by a potential buyer to purchase the property under stated terms.

Offset Statement

Statement by owner of property or owner of lien against property setting forth the present status of liens against said property.

Off-sale License

A liquor license issued by the ABC permitting the licensee to sell alcoholic beverages that are to be consumed off the premises.

Off-site Improvements

Improvements that add to the usefulness of the site but are not located directly on it such as, streets, sidewalks, sewers and lighting.

On-sale License

A liquor license issued by the ABC to establishments that sell alcoholic beverages for consumption on the premises.

Open-End Mortgage

A mortgage containing a clause which permits the mortgagor to borrow additional money after the loan has been reduced without rewriting the mortgage.

Open Housing Law

Congress passed a law in April 1968 which prohibits discrimination in the sale of real estate because of race, color, or religion of buyers.

Open Listing

An authorization given by a property owner to a real estate agent wherein said agent is given the nonexclusive right to secure a purchaser; open listings may be given to any number of agents without liability to compensate any except the one who first secures a buyer ready, willing and able to meet the terms of the listing, or secures the acceptance by the seller of a satisfactory offer.

Operating Expenses

Periodic expenditures necessary to maintain the property and continue the production of Effective Gross Income.

Opinion Of Title

An attorney's written evaluation of the condition of the title to a parcel of land after examination of the abstract of title.

Option

A right given for a consideration to purchase or lease a property upon specified terms within a specified time, without obligating the party who receives the right to exercise the right.

Optionee

The person who receives an option on property.

Optionor

The owner of the title who gives an option.

Oral Contract

A verbal agreement; one which is not reduced to writing.

Ordinance

A statute enacted by the legislative department of a city or county government.

Orientation

Placing a structure on its lot with regard to its exposure to the rays of the sun, prevailing winds, privacy from the street and protection from outside noises.

Original Contractor

A contractor who contracts directly with the owner of real estate.

Original License

A liquor license initially issued by the ABC – not a transfer of an existing license.

Or More Clause

A clause in a trust deed or note that permits the borrower to payoff the loan at an early date.

Ostensible Authority

That authority which a third person reasonably believes an agent possesses because of the acts or omissions of the principal.

Outlawed

A claim that can no longer by prosecuted due to expiration of the period permitted by the Statute of Limitations.

Overall Rate

A capitalization rate used in appraising income producing properties, expressed as a percentage, that provides for a *return on*, as well as a *return of*, the capital invested.

Overimprovement

An improvement which is not the highest and best use for the site on which it is placed by reason of excess size or cost.

Owner

The person who owns property and might be listing it. He or she has not sold the property, so would not yet be a "seller".

Ownership

The right of one or more persons to possess and use property to the exclusion of all others. A collection of rights to the use and enjoyment of property.

P

Package Mortgage

A type of mortgage used in home financing covering real property, improvements, and movable equipment/appliances.

Panic Selling

The illegal act of inducing the sale, lease or listing of residential property on the grounds of a loss in value will occur due to entry into the neighborhood of persons of another race, religion, ancestry or national origin. Also called *blockbusting*.

Paramount Title

Title which is superior or foremost to all others.

Parcel

Any area of land contained within one legal description.

Parol Contract

A spoken or oral contract. One not reduced to writing.

Partial Reconveyance Deed

The deed used to reconvey a portion of land encumbered by a trust deed or blanket mortgage.

Partial Release Clause

A clause in a trust deed or mortgage that releases part of the property from the trust deed or mortgage upon partial payment of the debt.

Participation

Sharing of an interest in a property by a lender. In addition to base interest on mortgage loans on income properties, a percentage of gross income is required, sometimes predicated on certain conditions being fulfilled, such as a minimum occupancy or percentage of net income after expenses, debt service and taxes. Also called equity partic ipation or revenue sharing.

Participation Loan

A loan in which the lender receives some portion of the ownership and profits.

Parties (Party)

Those entities taking part in a transaction as a principal, e.g., seller, buyer, or lender in a real estate transaction.

Partition

A division of real or personal property or the proceeds therefrom among co-owners.

Partition Action

Court proceedings by which co-owners seek to sever their joint ownership.

Partnership

A decision of the California Supreme Court has defined a partnership in the following terms: "A partnership as between partners themselves may be defined to be a contract of two or more persons to unite their property, labor or skill, or some of them, in prosecution of some joint or lawful business, and to share the profits in certain proportions." A voluntary association of two or more persons to carry on a business or venture on terms of mutual participation in profits and losses.

Party Wall

A wall erected on the line between two adjoining properties, which are under different ownership, for the use of both properties.

Par Value

Market value, nominal value.

Passive Activity Income

Income from real estate or other business in which an owner does not actively participate.

Patent

Conveyance of title to government land.

Payment Adjustment Date

With regard to an adjustable rate mortgage, the date the borrower's monthly principal and interest payment may change.

Payment Cap

With regard to an adjustable rate mortgage, this limits the amount of increase in the borrower's monthly principal and interest at the payment adjustment date, if the principal and interest increase called for by the interest rate increase exceeds the payment cap percentage. This limitation is often at the borrower's option and may result in negative amortization.

Payment Rate

With respect to an adjustable rate mortgage, the rate at which the borrower repays the loan-reflects buydowns or payment caps.

Pedestrian Count

A count of persons walking past a business location. The count is used in appraising the property for business purposes.

Penalty

An extra payment or charge required of the borrower for deviating from the terms of the original loan agreement. Usually levied for being late in making regular payment or for paying off the loan before it is due, known as "late charges" and "prepayment penalties."

Percentage Lease

Lease on the property, the rental for which is determined by amount of business done by the lessee; usually a percentage of gross receipts from the business with provision for a minimum rental.

Perimeter Heating

Baseboard heating, or any system in which the heat registers are located along the outside walls of a room, especially under the windows.

Periodic Interest Rate Cap

With respect to an adjustable rate mortgage, limits the increase or decrease in the note rate at each rate adjustment, thereby limiting the borrower's payment increase or decrease at the time of adjustment.

Per Se

As such, by itself, in itself, taken alone or unconnected with other matters.

Percentage

A given part or amount in every hundred.

Percolation

The ability of the soil to absorb water. Percolating water is subsurface water which a landowner may use.

Periodic Tenancy

Tenancy for successive periods of the same length unless terminated by proper notice of either party, for example, a month-to-month tenancy.

Personal Property

Any property which is not real property.

Personal Residence

A home in which the owner resides. For tax purposes a person may have multiple personal residences, but only one primary residence also called a domicile.

Physical Deterioration

Impairment of condition. Loss in value brought about by wear and tear, disintegration, use and actions of the elements; termed curable and incurable.

Physical Life

The estimated period during which a building can stand, as distinguished from its "economic life" the period in which it can produce income.

Plaintiff

In a court action, the one who sues; the complainant.

Planned Development

A subdivision consisting of separately owned parcels of land together with membership in an association which owns common area. Sometimes the owners of separate interests also have an undivided interest in the common area.

Planned Unit Development

(PUD) A term sometimes used to describe a planned development. A planning and zoning term describing land not subject to conventional zoning to permit clustering of residences or other characteristics of the project which differ from normal zoning.

Planning Commission

An agency of local government charged with planning the development, redevelopment or preservation of an area.

Plat (of survey)

A map of land made by a surveyor showing the boundaries, buildings, and other improvements.

Pledge

The depositing of personal property by a debtor with a creditor as security for a debt or engagement.

Pledgee

One who is given a pledge or a security. (See definition of Secured Party.)

Pledgor

One who offers a pledge or gives security. (See definition of debtor.)

Plot Plan

A plan showing the lot dimensions, boundaries and improvements drawn to scale. It may also include walks, driveways and roof plans of the various structures on the property.

Plottage

A term used in appraising to designate the increased value of two or more contiguous lots when they are joined under single ownership and available for use as a larger single lot. Also called assemblage.

Plottage Increment

The appreciation in unit value created by joining smaller ownerships into one large single ownership.

Plus Interest

A loan payment plan that calls for straight (or equal) principal reduction payments plus the accrued interest.

Points

See Discount Points.

Police Power

The right of the State to enact laws and enforce them for the order, safety, health, morals and general welfare of the public.

Potable

Water that is drinkable and not contaminated.

Power of Attorney

A written instrument whereby a principal gives authority to an agent. The agent acting under such a grant is sometimes called an attorney in fact.

Power of Sale

The power of a mortgagee or trustee when the instrument so provides to sell the secured property without judicial proceedings if a borrower defaults in payment of the promissory note or otherwise breaches the terms of the mortgage or deed of trust.

Prefabricated House

A house manufactured and sometimes partly assembled before delivery to building site.

Preferred Stock

A class of corporate stock entitled to preferential treatment such as priority in distribution of dividends.

Prepaid Items of Expense

Prorations of prepaid items of expense which are credited to the seller in the closing escrow statement.

Prepaid Interest

Interest paid before it has accrued or paid before the funds are available to the borrower.

Prepayment

Provision made for loan payments to be larger than those specified in the note.

Prepayment Penalty

The charge payable to a lender by a borrower under the terms of the loan agreement if the borrower pays off the outstanding principal balance of the loan prior to its maturity.

Prescription

The means of acquiring incorporeal interests in land, usually an easement, by immemorial or long continued use. The time is ordinarily the term of the statute of limitations.

Presumption

An assumption of fact that the law requires to be made from another fact or group of facts found or otherwise established in the section.

Prima Facie

Latin meaning first sight, a fact presumed to be true until disproved.

Primary Financing

The trust deed and note that has first priority.

Primary Mortgage Market

The market to which borrowers go to get loans that are made directly to them.

Principal

This term is used to mean the employer of an agent; or the amount of money borrowed, or the amount of the loan. Also, one of the main parties in a real estate transaction, such as a buyer, borrower, seller, lessor.

Principal Note

The promissory note which is secured by the mortgage or trust deed.

Prior Lien

A lien which is senior or superior to others.

Priority of Lien

The order in which liens are given legal precedence or preference.

Private Mortgage Insurance

Mortgage guaranty insurance available to conventional lenders on the first, high risk portion of a loan (PMI).

Private Restriction

A restriction placed on real property by the grantor.

Privity

Mutual relationship to the same rights of property, contractual relationship.

Privity of Contract

The relationship which exists between the persons who are parties to a contract.

Probate

A minimum four-month period during which the Superior Court has jurisdiction over the administration of the estate of all deceased persons in California whether they died testate (with a will) or intestate (without a will).

Probate Court

The Superior Court that has authority over the property of deceased persons, as well as minors and insane persons.

Procuring Cause

That cause originating from a series of events that, without break in continuity, results in the prime object of an agent's

Profit and Loss Statement

A financial report listing income and expenses, including depreciation and income tax deductions, showing profit or loss from operations over a given period of time – month, quarter or year.

Progressive Tax

A tax in which the tax rate increases as the taxable quantity increases such as, the federal income tax.

Promotional Note

A type of real property security. It is typified by the purchase-money second mortgages on a new subdivision before they become seasoned.

Property Manager

One who leases, maintains and manages property for others.

Property Residual Technique

An appraisal technique used in the income approach to estimate the total value of a property, including both land and improvements.

Prorate

To divide proportionately in time or use.

Public Report

The report of the Real Estate Commissioner under the Subdivided Lands Act, containing information about subdivided property.

Public Restriction

A government regulation limiting the use of real property.

Puffing

The unethical and illegal practice of making inflated or exaggerated statements that do not clearly represent the truth.

Purchase of Land, Leaseback and Leasehold Mortgages

An arrangement whereby land is purchased by the lender and leased back to the developer with a mortgage negotiated on the resulting leasehold of the income property constructed. The lender receives an annual ground rent, plus a percentage of income from the property.

Purchase and Leaseback

Involves the purchase of property by buyer and immediate leaseback to seller.

Purchase Money Mortgage or Trust Deed

A trust deed or mortgage given as part or all of the purchase consideration for real property. In some states the purchase money mortgage or trust deed loan can be made by a seller who extends credit to the buyer of property or by a third party lender (typically a financial institution) that makes a loan to the buyer of real property for a portion of the purchase price to be paid for the property. In many states there are legal limitations upon mortgagees and trust deed beneficiaries collecting deficiency judgments against the purchase money borrower after the collateral hypothecated under such security instruments has been sold through the foreclosure process. Generally no deficiency judgment is allowed if the collateral property under the mortgage or trust deed is residential property of four units or less with the debtor occupying the property as a place of residence.

Q

Quantity Survey

A highly technical process in arriving at cost estimate of new construction and sometimes referred to in the building trade as the "price take-off" method. It involves a detailed estimate of the quantities of raw material (lumber, plaster, brick, cement, etc.,) used as well as the current price of the material and installation costs. These factors are all added together to arrive at the cost of a structure. It is usually used by contractors and experienced estimators.

Quarter Round

A molding that presents a profile of a quarter circle.

Quiet Enjoyment

Right of an owner or tenant to the use of the property without interference of possession.

Quiet Title

A court action brought to establish title; to remove a cloud on the title.

Quitclaim Deed

A deed to relinquish any interest in property which the grantor may have, without any warranty of title or interest.

R

Radiant Heating

A method of heating, usually consisting of coils, or pipes placed in the floor, wall, or ceiling.

Range

A strip or column of land six miles wide, determined by a government survey, running in a north-south direction, lying east or west of a principal meridian.

Range Lines

A series of government survey lines running north and south at six-mile intervals starting with the principal meridian and forming the east and west boundaries of townships.

Rate Adjustment Date

With respect to an adjustable rate mortgage, the date the borrower's note rate may change.

Ratification

The adoption or approval of an act performed on behalf of a person without previous authorization, such as the approval by a principal of previously unauthorized acts of an agent, after the acts have been performed.

Ready, Willing and Able Buyer

One who is fully prepared to enter into the contract, really wants to buy, and unquestionably meets the financing requirements of purchase.

Real Estate

(See Real Property.)

Real Estate Board

An organization whose members consist primarily of real estate brokers and salespersons.

Real Estate Commissioner

The head of the Department of Real Estate.

Real Estate Fund

The fund for the operation of the Department of Real Estate funded by license fees. It includes the Education and Research Fund and the Recovery Account.

Real Estate Investment Trust

(See REIT).

Real Estate Settlement Procedures Act (RESPA)

A federal law requiring the disclosure to borrowers of settlement (closing) procedures and costs by means of a pamphlet and forms prescribed by the United States Department of Housing and Urban Development.

Real Estate Syndicate

An organization of investors usually in the form of a limited partnership who have joined together for the purpose of pooling capital for the acquisition of real property interests.

Real Estate Trust

A special arrangement under Federal and State law whereby investors may pool funds for investments in real estate and mortgages and yet escape corporation taxes, profits being passed to individual investors who are taxed.

Real Property

In the strict legal sense, land appurtenances, that which is affixed to the land, and that which by law is immovable. It usually refers to the "bundle of rights" inherent in ownership.

Real Property Loan Law

Article 7 of Chapter 3 of the Real Estate Law under which a real estate licensee negotiating loans secured by real property within a specified range is required to give the borrower a statement disclosing the costs and terms of the loan and which also limits the amount of expenses and charges that a borrower may pay with respect to the loan.

Real Property Sales Contract

An agreement to convey title to real property upon satisfaction of specified conditions which does not require conveyance within one year of formation of the contract.

Real Property Securities

A term for certain types of real estate paper subject to special regulation when sold to the public–guaranteed or promotional notes and sales contracts and out of state subdivision lots sold or leased in California.

Real Property Securities Dealer

A real estate broker whose license has been endorsed to permit selling guaranteed real property securities.

Realized Gain

Also called actual gain and results from the sale of a capital asset. This is the total of both recognized and deferred gain.

Realtist

A real estate broker holding active membership in a real estate board affiliated with the National Association of Real Estate Brokers.

Realtor®

Registered trademark of the National Association of Realtors®, its state associations and local boards. Some jurisdictions make a distinction between Realtors® (who must be licensed as real estate brokers) and Realtor-Associates® (who hold sales licenses). Others designate all of their members as Realtors®.

Recapture

The process of recovery by an owner of money invested by employing the use of a rate of interest necessary to provide for the return of an investment; not to be confused with interest rate, which is a rate of return on an investment.

Reclamation

Any method for bringing waste natural resources again into productive use.

Recognized Gain

Gain that is taxable in the year of the transaction.

Reconciliation

The same as correlation–bringing together estimates from the sales comparison, cost, and income approaches to generate a final estimate of value.

Reconveyance

The transfer of the title of land from one person to the immediate preceding owner. This instrument of transfer is commonly used to transfer the legal title from the trustee to the trustor (borrower) after a trust deed debt has been paid in full.

Recordation

A system by which documents concerning title and other legal matters are collected in one convenient, public place, commonly the county recorder's office. Documents properly recorded constitute constructive notice of the contents of the documents.

Recording

The process of placing a document on file with a designated public official for public notice. This public official is usually a county officer known as the County Recorder who designates the fact that a document has been presented for recording by placing a recording stamp upon it indicating the time of day and the date when it was officially placed on file. Documents filed with the Recorder are considered to be placed on open notice to the general public of that county. Claims against property usually are given a priority on the basis of the time and the date they are recorded with the most preferred claim going to the earliest one recorded and the next claim going to the next earliest one recorded, and so on. This type of notice is called "constructive notice" or "legal notice".

Recorded Map

Under the Subdivision Map Act, a map must be recorded in the county where a property is located in order to create new legal parcels. This allows the use of the Recorded Map Method (Lot & Block) of formal legal descriptions.

Recovery Account

Part of the Real Estate Fund held by the Department of Real Estate to underwrite uncollectable court judgments against licensees for fraud, misrepresentation, and similar acts.

Recurring Costs

Expenses that an owner can expect year after year, such as property taxes, fire insurance, and interest.

Redeem

To buy back; repurchase; recover.

Redemption

Buying back one's property after a judicial sale.

Redevelopment

Renewal of a blighted area, such as by clearing slums and erecting new buildings or by rehabilitating existing buildings.

Redlining

A lending policy, illegal in California, of denying real estate loans on properties in older, changing urban areas, usually with large minority populations, because of alleged higher lending risks without due consideration being given by the lending institution to the credit worthiness of the individual loan applicant.

Refinancing

The paying-off of an existing obligation and assuming a new obligation in its place. To finance anew, or extend or renew existing financing.

Reformation

An action to correct a mistake in a deed or other document.

Regression

An appraisal principle that holds that a higher valued property in a neighborhood of lower valued properties seeks the level of the lower valued properties. The opposite principle is progression.

Regulation Z

The Federal Reserve regulation that implements the Federal Consumer Credit Protection Act of 1969 or Truth in Lending law.

Rehabilitation

The restoration of a property to satisfactory condition without drastically changing the plan, form or style of architecture.

Reinstatement

The statutory right of a borrower to pay up a loan that has gone into default and return it to good standing, prior to the scheduled public auction of the property.

REIT

A Real Estate Investment Trust is a business trust which deals principally with interest in land- generally organized to conform to the Internal Revenue Code.

Release Clause

A stipulation that upon the payment of a specific sum of money to the holder of a trust deed or mortgage, the lien of the instrument as to a specifically described lot or area shall be removed from the blanket lien on the whole area involved.

Release Deed

An instrument executed by the mortgagee or the trustee reconveying to the mortgagor or trustor the real estate which secured the loan after the debt has been paid in full.

Release Statement

The form prescribed by the Uniform Commercial Code for indicating the release of all or part of a security interest.

Reliction

A gradual permanent recession or withdrawal of water from its usual sea or river watermark which results in an increase of land.

Remainder

An estate which takes effect after the termination of the prior estate, such as a life estate. A future possessory interest in real estate.

Remainder Depreciation

The possible future loss in value of an improvement to real property.

Remaining Economic Life

The period of time from the date of the appraisal to the date when the improvements will no longer add value to the land.

Remodeling

Changing the plan, form or style of a structure.

Renegotiable Rate Mortgage

A loan secured by a long term mortgage which provides for renegotiation, at pre-determined intervals, of the interest rate (for a maximum variation of five percent over the life of the mortgage.)

Rent

Consideration paid for the use and possession of a property for a certain, fixed or determinable length of time.

Replacement Cost

The cost to replace a structure with one having utility equivalent to that being appraised, but constructed with modern materials and according to current standards, design and layout.

Replevin

A legal action brought to recover possession of personal property wrongfully taken.

Reproduction Cost

The cost of replacing the subject improvement with one that is the exact replica, having the same quality of workmanship, design and layout, or cost to duplicate an asset.

Request for Notice of Default

A notice recorded by any interested party such as the beneficiary of a trust deed, requesting notification if foreclosure proceedings are started.

Rescission

The cancellation of a contract and restoration of the parties to the same position they held before the contract was entered into.

Rescission of Contract

The abrogation or annulling of contract; the revocation or repealing of contract by mutual consent by parties to the contract, or for cause by either party to the contract.

Reservation

A right retained by a grantor in conveying property.

Reserves

1) In a common interest subdivisions, an accumulation of funds collected from owners for future replacement and major maintenance of the common area and facilities. 2) With regard to mortgage loans, an accumulation of funds, collected by the lender from the borrower as part of each monthly mortgage payment, an amount allocated to pay property taxes and insurance when they are due.

Residence

A personal residence is where one lives, a home or place of abode, also called one's domicile. A person can have more than one personal residence.

Resident Manager

An agent of the owner of a building who is employed on a salary to manage the property in which the manager *resides*.

Residential

Primarily a zoning code classification but also pertaining to one's home and to housing in general.

Residential Purchase Agreement and Receipt for Deposit

The formal name for the "*deposit receipt*" used when accepting "*earnest money*" from a prospective purchaser with an offer to buy property.

RESPA

(See Real Estate Settlement Procedures Act.)

Restoration

Returning a building to its *original form.*

Restricted License

A probationary real estate license that contains specific restrictions.

Restriction

A limitation on the use of real property. Property restrictions fall into two general classifications-public and private. Zoning ordinances are examples of the former type. Restrictions may be created by private owners, typically by appropriate clauses in deeds, or in agreements, or in general plans of entire subdivisions. Usually they assume the form of a covenant, or promise to do or not to do a certain thing.

Retrospective Value

The value of the property as of a previous date.

Return

Profit from an investment; the yield.

Return of Investment

A recapture of investment either from sale or through depreciation. In appraisal an allowance for return of an investment of capital is termed an accrual for future depreciation.

Return on Investment

The interest or profit earned from an investment.

Reversion

The right to future possession or enjoyment by a person, or the person's heirs, creating the preceding estate. (For example, at the end of a lease.)

Reversionary Interest

The interest which a person has in lands or other property, upon the termination of the preceding estate. A future interest.

Revocation

The withdrawal or nullification of an offer to contract or a cancelling or the annulment of a license.

Rider

An addition, amendment or endorsement to a document.

Right of Survivorship

The right of a surviving tenant or tenants to succeed to the entire interest of the deceased tenant; the distinguishing feature of a joint tenancy.

Right of Way

A privilege operating as an easement upon land, whereby the owner does by grant, or by agreement, give to another the right to pass over owner's land, to construct a roadway, or use as a roadway, a specific part of the land; or the right to construct through and over the land, telephone, telegraph, or electric power lines; or the right to place underground water mains, gas mains, or sewer mains.

Right, Title and Interest

A term used in deeds to denote that the grantor is conveying all of that to which grantor held claim.

Right to Rescind

A right to terminate a contract unilaterally or by one side.

Riparian Rights

The right of a landowner whose land borders on a stream or watercourse to use and enjoy the water which is adjacent to or flows over the owners land provided such use does not injure other riparian owners.

Risk Analysis

A study made, usually by a lender, of the various factors that might affect the repayment of a loan.

Risk Rating

A process used by the lender to decide on the soundness of making a loan and to reduce all the various factors affecting the repayment of the loan to a qualified rating of some kind.

S

Sale and Leaseback

A financial arrangement where at the time of sale the seller retains occupancy by concurrently agreeing to lease the property from the purchaser. The seller receives cash while the buyer is assured a tenant and a fixed return on buyer's investment.

Sale-Leaseback-Buy-Back

A sale and leaseback transaction in which the leaseholder has the option to buy back the original property after a specified period of time.

Sales and Use Tax

Tax on the sale or use of certain tangible (touchable) personal property.

Sales Comparison Approach

Recent sales and listings of similar type properties in the area are analyzed to form an opinion of value. Previously called the market approach.

Sales Contract

A contract by which buyer and seller agree to terms of a sale.

Salesperson

A *natural person* who for compensation or in expectation of compensation, is employed by a licensed real estate broker to do one or more acts specified in the Real Estate Law. The Real Estate Law recognizes the terms salesman, saleswoman, and salesperson.

Rollover of Gain

A deferral of gain from the sale of one personal residence to another.

Salvage Value

In computing depreciation for tax purposes, the reasonably anticipated fair market value of the property at the end of its useful life and must be considered with all but the declining balance methods of depreciation.

Sandwich Lease

A leasehold interest which lies between the primary lease and the operating lease.

Sash

Wood or metal frames containing one or more window panes.

Satisfaction

Discharge of a mortgage or trust deed from the records upon payment of the debt.

Satisfaction Piece

An instrument for recording and acknowledging payment of an indebtedness secured by a mortgage.

Savings Association Insurance Fund

A fund managed by the FDIC that insures deposits in savings and loans. The successor to the former FSLIC.

SBB&M

The abbreviation for San Bernardino Base and Meridian.

Scarcity

An inadequate supply which can not easily be increased. Scarcity results in increased value when demand exceeds supply.

Scribing

Fitting woodwork to an irregular surface.

Seal

An impression made to attest the execution of an instrument.

Seasoned Loan

A loan with a good payment record.

Secondary Financing

A loan secured by a second mortgage or trust deed on real property. These can be third, fourth, fifth, sixth mortgages or trust deeds, on and on ad infinitum.

Secondary Mortgage Market

The market for the sale and purchase of existing trust deeds and mortgages.

Section

Section of land is established by government survey, contains 640 acres and is one mile square.

Secured

A lien for which a specific property is available to satisfy the debt if the borrower does not pay.

Secured Party

This is the party having the security interest. Thus the mortgagee, the conditional seller, the pledgee, etc., are all now referred to as the secured party. (Uniform Commercial Code.)

Security Agreement

An agreement between the secured party and the debtor which creates the security interest. (Uniform Commercial Code.)

Security Device

An instrument used to secure the payment of a loan. It may be a mortgage, trust deed, real property sales contract or a security agreement.

Security Interest

A term designating the interest of the creditor in the property of the debtor in all types of credit transactions. It thus replaces such terms as the following chattel mortgage; pledge; trust receipt; chattel trust; equipment trust; conditional sale; inventory lien; etc., according to Uniform Commercial Code usage.

Seisin (Seizin)

Possession of real estate by one entitled thereto.

Seller Financing Disclosure

Specific disclosures must be made by the *arranger of credit* to both seller and buyer where there is a transaction involving a purchase money lien on dwellings for not more than 4 families with the seller extending credit to the purchaser.

Seller's Market

The market condition which exists when a seller is in a more commanding position as to price and terms because demand exceeds supply.

Seller's Permit

A resale certificate obtained from the State Board of Equalization, required of all sellers of taxable goods in the state of California. The seller may be required to give a security deposit to the state to insure the payment of collected sales taxes.

Selling Agent

The licensee who procures a buyer for a property. Do not confuse with the seller's agent who is normally the listing agent.

Send-out Slip

A form enumerating listed properties or business opportunities that gets signed by the buyer who promises to buy through the issuing broker's office if the buyer purchases or leases one of the specified properties.

Separate Property

Property owned by a married person in his or her own right outside of the community interest including property acquired by the spouse (1) before marriage, (2) by gift or inheritance, (3) from rents and profits on separate property, and (4) with the proceeds from other separate property.

Septic Tank

An underground tank in which sewage from the house is reduced to liquid by bacterial action and drained off.

Service

The process of collecting payments after a loan has been made, handling late charges, foreclosure, etc. Not necessarily done by the same agency that administered the loan.

Servicing Loans

Supervising and administering a loan after it has been made. This involves such things as collecting the payments, keeping accounting records, computing the interest and principal, foreclosure of defaulted loans, and so on.

Servient Tenement

Land burdened by an easement.

Set Back Ordinance

An ordinance requiring improvements built on property to be a specified distance from the property line, street or curb.

Set-off

A right that exists between two parties, each of whom under a separate contract owes the other a certain amount of money, by which they may *set off* their respective debts by a mutual deduction.

Severalty Ownership

Owned by one person only. Sole ownership.

Shared Appreciation Mortgage

A loan having a fixed rate of interest set below the market rate for the term of the loan which also provides for contingent interest to be paid to the lender on a certain percentage of appreciation in the value of the property against which the loan is secured upon transfer or sale of the property or the repayment of the loan.

Sheriff's Deed

Deed given by court order in connection with sale of property to satisfy a judgment.

Short Rate

The higher periodic rate that is charged for a shorter term than that originally contracted for when an insured cancels a policy.

Short-term Capital Gain

Gain on sale of property owned for less than one year. Gain is fully taxed and loss is fully deductible.

Simple Interest

Interest computed on the principal amount of a loan only as distinguished from compound interest.

Sinking Fund

Fund set aside from the income from property which, with accrued interest, will eventually pay for replacement of the improvements.

Site

The area or the place on which anything is, has been or is to be located.

Slander of Title

False and malicious statements disparaging an owner's title to property and resulting in actual pecuniary damage to the owner.

Social Obsolescence

A loss in value of property due to incurable factors outside the property–the same as economic obsolescence.

Soil Pipe

The pipe carrying waste water from the house to the main sewer line.

Soldiers' and Sailors' Civil Relief Act

A federal law providing protection against foreclosure to an individual, while in the service, who contracted for an obligation before entry into the service.

Special Assessment

1) Legal charge against real estate by a public authority to pay cost of public improvements such as street lights, sidewalks, street improvements. 2) In a common interest subdivision, a charge, in addition to the regular assessment, levied by the association against owners in the development, for unanticipated repairs or maintenance on the common area or capital improvement of the common area.

Special Power of Attorney

A written instrument whereby a principal confers limited authority upon an agent to perform certain prescribed acts on behalf of the principal.

Special Warranty Deed

A deed in which the grantor warrants or guarantees the title only against defects arising during grantor's ownership of the property and not against defects existing before the time of grantor's ownership.

Specific Performance

An action to compel performance of an agreement, e.g., sale of land as an alternative to damages or rescission.

Spendable Income

The money remaining from gross income after deducting operating expenses, principal and interest payments and income tax. Also called net spendable.

SREA

Society of Real Estate Appraisers.

Standard Depth

Generally the most typical lot depth in the neighborhood.

Standard Form

The basic title insurance policy usually issued by the California Land Title Association (CLTA) to a purchaser of real property which provides coverage against forgery and fraud, matters of record, improper delivery, and lack of capacity.

Standard Subdivision

A subdivision in which there are no common areas and no lien rights. Subdividers selling urban homes, and not land in one of these subdivisions do not have to comply with the Subdivided Lands Law.

Standby Commitment

The mortgage banker frequently protects a builder by a "standby" agreement, under which banker agrees to make mortgage loans at an agreed price for many months into the future. The builder deposits a "standby fee" with the mortgage banker for this service. Frequently, the mortgage broker protects self by securing a "standby" from a long-term investor for the same period of time, paying a fee for this privilege.

State Housing Law

The state law that sets minimum building standards throughout the state of California.

Statute of Frauds

A state law, based on an old English statute, requiring certain contracts to be in writing and signed before they will be enforceable at law, e.g. contracts for the sale of real property, contracts not be performed within one year.

Statute of Limitations

The law that specifies the time limits within which any legal action must be begun.

Statutory Dedication

The giving of private land for public use under a procedure established by statute.

Statutory Warranty Deed

A short term warranty deed which warrants by inference that the seller is the undisputed owner, has the right to convey the property, and will defend the title if necessary. This type of deed protects the purchaser in that the conveyor covenants to defend all claims against the property. If conveyor fails to do so, the new owner can defend said claims and sue the former owner.

Stock Cooperative

A multiple unit property owned by a corporation, in which each stockholder has exclusive right of occupancy through a Proprietary Lease in a portion of the property.

Stock-in-Trade

Merchandise held by a business for sale.

Straight Line Depreciation

A method of depreciation under which improvements are depreciated at a constant rate throughout the estimated useful life of the improvement.

Straight Line Equation

A three-quantity equation in which the three quantities have a fixed mathematical rela tion, so that given any two, the third can be found. The simplest example of a straight line equation is "2 times 3 equals 6."

Straight Note

A note in which a borrower repays the principal in a lump sum at maturity while interest is paid in installments or at maturity. (See Interest Only Note.)

Street Improvement Act of 1911

The California law that authorizes local governing bodies to order street improvements and bill the owners for the work or to pay the costs through a bond issue and have the owners pay off the bond through a special assessment.

Subagent

A person upon whom the powers of an agent have been conferred, not by the principal, but by an agent as authorized by the agent's principal.

Subdivided Lands Act

A California law regulating the division of land into five or more parcels of less than 160 acres or five or more undivided interests of any size. It is administered by the Real Estate Commissioner.

Subdivision

A legal definition of those divisions of real property for the purpose of sale, lease or financing which are regulated by law. For examples see California Business and Professions Code Sections 11000, 11000.1, 11004.5; California Government Code Section 66424; United States Code, Title 15, Section 1402(3).

Subdivision Map Act

A California law authorizing local governments to regulate the physical aspects of subdivisions.

Subjacent Support

The support that the surface of the earth receives from the land that lies under it.

"Subject To" A Mortgage

When a grantee takes title to real property subject to a mortgage, grantee is not responsible to the holder of the promissory note for the payment of any portion of the amount due. The. most that grantee can lose in the event of a foreclosure is grantee's equity in the property. (See also "assumption of mortgage".) In neither case is the original maker of the note released from primary responsibility. If liability is to be assumed, the agreement must so state.

Sublease

A lease given by a lessee.

Subordinate

To make subject to, or junior or inferior to.

Subordination Agreement

An agreement by the holder of an encumbrance against real property to permit that claim to take an inferior position to other encumbrances against the property.

Subpoena

A legal order to cause a witness to appear and give testimony.

Subrogation

Replacing one person with another in regard to a legal right or obligation. The substitution of another person in place of the creditor, to whose rights he or she succeeds in relation to the debt. The doctrine is used very often where one person agrees to stand surety for the performance of a contract by another person.

Subsidy Buydown

Funds provided usually by the builder or seller to temporarily reduce the borrower's monthly principal and interest payment.

Substitution of Mortgagor

An agreement signed by the lender on a loan that is being assumed by a buyer, whereby the lender relieves the original borrower of all liability.

Substitution, Principle of

Affirms that the maximum value of a property tends to be set by the cost of acquiring an equally desirable and valuable substitute property, assuming no costly delay is encountered in making the substitution.

Succession

Transfer of property under the laws of inheritance when a person dies without a will (intestate).

Successor

One who follows or comes after, such as the buyer of a business who becomes the seller's successor.

Successor's Liability

The liability that a purchaser of a business might have for nonpayment of sales taxes by the previous owner.

Sufferance

The interest that exists when a tenant holds over without the consent of the landlord after the expiration of a lease. Also called estate at sufferance.

Sum of the Years Digits

An accelerated depreciation method.

Summary Proceeding

A short, concise and immediate legal proceeding without a jury. An Unlawful Detainer Action is an example of a summary proceeding.

Supply and Demand, Principle of

In appraising, a valuation principle starting that market value is affected by intersection of supply and demand forces in the market as of the appraisal date.

Surety

One who guarantees the performance of another guarantor.

Surface Water

Water resulting from rains and melting snows that is diffused over the surface of the ground. An owner may not divert surface water onto the land of another without their permission.

Surplus Productivity, Principle of

The net income that remains after the proper costs of labor, organization and capital have been paid, which surplus is imputable to the land and tends to fix the value thereof.

Surrender

Giving up a lease before its expiration date.

Survey

The process by which a parcel of land is measured and its area is ascertained.

Suspension

A temporary cancellation of a license.

Syndicate

A partnership organized for participation in a real estate venture. Partners may be limited or unlimited in their liability. (See real estate syndicate.)

T

Take-Out Loan

The loan arranged by the owner or builder developer for a buyer. The construction loan made for construction of the improvements is usually paid in full from the proceeds of this more permanent mortgage loan.

Tangible

Property that can be physically touched or handled such as stock-in-trade.

Tax

Enforced charge exacted of persons, corporations and organizations by the government to be used to support government services and programs.

Tax Deed

The deed given to a purchaser at a public sale of land held for nonpayment of taxes. It conveys to the purchaser only such title as the defaulting taxpayer had.

Tax-Free Exchange

The trade or exchange of one real property for another without the need to pay income taxes on the gain at the time of trade.

Taxpayer Relief Act of 1997

Made significant changes in capital gain provisions. Exclusion from capital gain ($250,000) for sale of principal residence every two years. Eliminated the "rollover" provision and the senior exemption. Made changes in long- term capital gain treatment.

Tax Rate

A set percentage times a taxable value which is used to calculate an amount of tax.

Tax Reform Act of 1986

The Internal Revenue Code of 1986 which replaced the previous code of 1954.

Tax Sale

Sale of property after a period of nonpayment of taxes.

Tenancy

The mode of holding property, such as a joint tenancy, tenancy in common or tenancy for years.

Tenancy In Common

Co-ownership of property by two or more persons who hold undivided interest, without right of survivorship; interests need not be equal.

Tenant

The party who has legal possession and use of real property belonging to another.

Tenantability

Fit to live in, according to a specific list of items in the Civil Code.

Tenants By The Entireties

Under certain state laws, ownership of property acquired by a husband and wife during marriage, which property is jointly and equally owned. Upon depth of one spouse it becomes the property of the survivor.

Tender

An unconditional offer of money or performance. When unjustifiably refused, it may permit the party making tender to exercise remedies for breach of contract.

Tenement

All rights in land which pass with a conveyance of the land.

Tentative Map

The Subdivision Map Act requires subdividers to submit initially a tentative map of their tract to the local planning commission for study. The approval or disapproval of the planning commission is noted on the map. Thereafter, a final map of the tract embodying any changes requested by the planning commission is required to be filed with the planning commission.

Tenure In Land

The mode or manner by which an estate in lands is held. All rights and title rest with owner.

Termination Statement

The document recorded to cancel and remove a financing statement previously filed under the Uniform Commercial Code.

Termites

Ant-like insects which feed on wood and are highly destructive to wooden structures.

Termite Shield

A shield, usually of noncorrodible metal, placed on top of the foundation wall or around pipes to prevent passage of termites.

Testament

The written declaration of one's last will.

Testate

Dying and leaving a will–the opposite of intestate–leaving no will.

Testator

One who makes a will.

Testatrix

A term sometimes used for a woman who makes a will.

Third Party

Persons who are not parties to a contract which affects an interest they have in the object of the contract.

Threshold

A strip of wood or metal beveled on each edge and used above the finished floor under outside doors.

Tier

A row of townships running east and west and lying between any two consecutive township lines and comprising an area six miles wide.

Tidelands

Lands that are covered and uncovered by the ebb and flow of the tide.

Tight Money Market

A situation where loan funds are scarce and interest rates and discount points are high.

Time Is Of The Essence

A condition of a contract expressing the essential nature of performance of the contract by a party in a specified period of time.

Time-share Estate

A right of occupancy in a time- share project (subdivision) which is coupled with an estate in the real property.

Time-Share Project

A form of subdivision of real property into rights to the recurrent, exclusive use or occupancy of a lot, parcel, unit, or segment of real property, on an annual or some other periodic basis, for a specified period of time.

Time-Share Use

A license or contractual or membership right of occupancy in a timeshare project which is not coupled with an estate in the real property.

Title

Indicates "fee" position of lawful ownership and right to property. "Bundle of Rights" possessed by an owner. Combination of all elements constituting proof of ownership.

Title Insurance

Insurance to protect a real property owner or lender up to a specified amount against certain types of loss, e.g., defective or unmarketable title.

Title Plant

The storage facility of a title insurance company containing a complete set of title records of properties in its area.

Title Report

A report which discloses condition of the title, made by a title company preliminary to issuance of title insurance policy.

Title Theory

Mortgage arrangement whereby title to mortgaged real property vests in the lender. Some states give greater protection to mortgage lenders and assume lenders have title interest. Distinguished from Lien Theory States.

Topography

Nature of the surface of land; topography may be level, rolling, mountainous. Variation in earth's surface.

Torrens System

A legal system of land registration without the need for additional search of public records formerly used in California.

Torrens Title

System of title records provided by state law (no longer used in California)

Tort

Any wrongful act (not involving a breach of contract) for which a civil section will lie for the person wronged.

Townhouse

One of a row of houses usually of the same or similar design with common side walls or with a very narrow space between adjacent side walls.

Township

In the survey of public lands of the United States, a territorial subdivision six miles long, six miles wide and containing 36 sections, each one mile square, located between two range lines and two township lines.

Trade Fixtures

Articles of personal property annexed by a business tenant to real property which are necessary to the carrying on of a trade and are removable by the tenant.

Trade-In

An increasingly popular method of guaranteeing an owner a minimum amount of cash on sale of owner's present property to permit owner to purchase another. If the property is not sold within a specified time at the listed price, the broker agrees to arrange financing to personally purchase the property at an agreed upon discount.

Trade Name

The name under which a company carries on business.

Trading on Equity

Borrowing funds at interest rates lower than the earning rate of the property.

Transferability

Potential for being conveyed from one owner to another. Transferability is one of the four essential elements of value.

Transfer Fee

A charge made by a lending institution holding or collecting on a real estate mortgage to change its records to reflect a different ownership.

Trend

An appraisal term for a series of related events brought about by a chain of predictable causes and effects.

Trust Account

An account separate and apart and physically segregated from broker's own funds, in which broker is required by law to deposit all funds collected for clients.

Trust Deed

Just as with a mortgage this is a legal document by which a borrower pledges certain real property or collateral as guarantee for the repayment of a loan. However, it differs from the mortgage in a number of important respects. For example, instead of there being two parties to the transaction there are three. There is the borrower who signs the trust deed and who is called the trustor. There is the third, neutral party, to whom trustor deeds the property as security for the payment of the debt, who is called the trustee. And, finally, there is the lender who is called the beneficiary, the one who benefits from the pledge agreement in that in the event of a default the trustee can sell the property and transfer the money obtained at the sale to lender as payment of the debt.

Trust Funds

A collective term for money or things of value received by a broker or salesperson on behalf of and for the benefit of the principal.

Trust Ledger

A record of all trust funds received such as cash or checks whether placed in the broker's trust account, given to the seller or placed in escrow.

Trustee

One who holds property in trust for another to secure the performance of an obligation. Third party under a deed of trust.

Trustee's Deed

The deed given when property is sold under the power of sale in a trust deed.

Trustor

One who borrows money from a trust deed lender, then deeds the real property securing the loan to a trustee to be held as security until trustor has performed the obligation to the lender under terms of a deed of trust.

Truth In Lending

The name given to the federal statutes and regulations (Regulation Z) which are designed primarily to insure that prospective borrowers and purchasers on credit receive credit cost information before entering into a transaction.

Turnover

The number of times a given amount of inventory sells over a given period of time.

U

Underimprovement

An improvement which, because of its deficiency in size or cost, is not the highest and best use of the site.

Underwriting

Insuring something against loss; guaranteeing financially.

Undue Influence

Use of a fiduciary or confidential relationship to obtain a fraudulent or unfair advantage over another's weakness of mind, or distress or necessity.

Unearned Increment

An increase in value of real estate due to no effort on the part of the owner; often due to increase in population.

Undivided Interest

The separate interest of each co- owner in an entire property. Each interest is indistinguishable which means that a co-owner does not own a specified separate part of the property but owns an *unspecified interest in the whole.*

Unenforceable

A law or contract that a person can not be compelled to observe.

Uniform Commercial Code

Establishes a unified and comprehensive method for regulation of security transactions in personal property, superseding the existing statutes on chattel mortgages, conditional sales, trust receipts, assignment of accounts receivable and others in this field.

Uniform Settlement Statement

The standard RESPA Form or HUD-1 required to be given to the borrower, lender and seller at or before settlement by the settlement agent in a transaction covered by RESPA.

Uniform Vendor and Purchaser Risk Act

A California law providing that transfer of title or possession is the determining fact in the question of risk of loss by flood, earthquake, fire, etc.

Unilateral

Done by, undertaken by or obligating only one side. A unilateral contract is binding on one side only such as when a *promise* is made in exchange for an *act.*

Unit-In-Place Method

The cost of erecting a building by estimating the cost of each component part, i.e., foundations, floors, walls, windows, ceilings, roofs, etc., (including labor and overhead).

Unlawful Detainer

A legal action to evict a tenant who unlawfully remains in possession of real property originally rightfully obtained. The owner of the property is unlawfully detained from using their property.

Unruh Civil Rights Act

The California law prohibiting discrimination by business establishments because of race, creed, color or national origin.

Unsecured

A lien for which no specific property stands as security to satisfy the debt.

Urban Property

City property; closely settled property.

U.S. Department of Veterans Affairs

Department of Veterans Affairs is the federal government agency that administers GI or VA loans. Previously known as the Veterans Administration or VA.

USPAP

The Uniform Standards of Professional Appraisal Practice is a code governing licensed and certified appraisers. This code guides appraisers in the development of the appraisal process and the content of the report. The code is developed and modified (promulgated) by the Appraisal Foundation.

Usury

On a loan, claiming a rate of interest greater than that permitted by law.

Utilities

Refers to services rendered by public utility companies, such as water, gas, electricity, telephone.

Utility

The ability to give satisfaction and/or excite desire for possession. An element of value.

V

Vacancy Factor

The percentage of a building's space that is not rented over a given period.

Valid

Having force, or binding force; legally sufficient and authorized by law.

Valley

The internal angle formed by the junction of two sloping sides of a roof.

Valuation

Estimated worth or price. Estimation. The act of valuing by appraisal.

VA Loan

A loan made to qualified veterans for the purchase of real property wherein the Department of Veteran's Affairs guarantees the lender payment of the mortgage.

Variance

Legal permission to build a structure or use a property in a way that does not conform to the current zoning laws. It is not a change in the zoning.

Value

Present worth of future benefits arising out of ownership to typical users/investors.

Variable Interest Rate

(VIRs or VMRs, Variable Mortgage Rates.) An interest rate in a real estate loan which by the terms of the note varies upward and downward over the term of the loan depending on money market conditions.

Vendee

A purchaser; buyer.

Vendor

A seller.

Veneer

Thin sheets of wood.

Verification

Sworn statement before a duly qualified officer to correctness of contents of an instrument.

Vested

Bestowed upon someone; secured by someone, such as title to property.

Veterans Tax Exemption

An exemption as provided by state law of $4,000 on the assessed value of a veteran's property.

Void

To have no force or effect; that which is unenforceable.

Voidable

That which is capable of being adjudged void, but is not void unless action is taken to make it so.

Voluntary Lien

Any lien placed on property with consent of, or as a result of, the voluntary act of the owner.

W

Wainscoting

Wood lining of an interior wall; lower section of a wall when finished differently from the upper part.

Waive

To relinquish, or abandon; to forego a right to enforce or require anything.

Waiver

The intentional or voluntary relinquishment of a known right, essentially a unilateral act.

Walk-up

An apartment of more than one story that does not have an elevator. As the term implies, the tenant must walk up the stairs to get to the apartment.

Warehousing

The holding of loan portfolios by a primary lender pending sale in the secondary mortgage market.

Warranty of Authority

A representation by an agent to third persons that the agent has and is acting within the scope of authority conferred by his or her principal.

Warranty Deed

A deed used to convey real property which contains warranties of title and quiet possession, and the grantor thus agrees to defend the premises against the lawful claims of third persons. It is commonly used in many states but in others the grant deed has supplanted it due to the modern practice of securing title insurance policies which have reduced the importance of express and implied warranty in deeds.

Waste

The destruction, or material alteration of, or injury to premises by a tenant.

Water Table

Distance from surface of ground to a depth at which natural groundwater is found.

Wear and Tear

Depreciation of an asset due to ordinary usage.

Wild Document

A document either created by a "stranger to the title," such as a forger or made "outside the chain of title," such as a conveyance granted by someone who previously failed to record and thereby left a link missing in the chain of title.

Will

A written, legal declaration of a person expressing his or her desires for the disposition of that person's property after his or her death.

Wrap Around Mortgage

A financing device whereby a lender assumes
  payments on existing trust deeds of a borrower
  and takes from the borrower a junior trust deed
  with a face value in an amount equal to the
  amount outstanding on the old trust deeds and
the additional amount of money borrowed.

Writ of Execution

A writ or writing to carry out the judgment or
  decree of a court, for example that a property
  be sold to satisfy a debt.

X

X

An individual who cannot write may execute a
legal document by affixing an "X"
  (his/her mark) where the signature normally
  goes. Beneath the mark a witness then writes
  the person's name and signs his or her own
  name as witness.

Y

Yard

A unit of measurement 3 feet long.

Yield

The interest earned by an investor on an
  investment, also called return.

Yield Capitalization

An income approach method of estimating value
  used for commercial property. In this method,
  the appraiser uses several years' income and
  the reversion from the sale, discounted to
  present value. In direct capitalization, only one
  year's income is considered. An appraiser
  would not rely on yield capitalization only.

Yield Rate

The yield expressed as a percentage of the total
  investment. Also, called rate of return.

Z

Zone

The area set off by the proper authorities for
  specific use; an area subject to certain
  restrictions or restraints.

Zoning

Act of city or county authorities specifying type
  of use to which property may be put in
  specific areas.